Cliffs and Challenges

Cliffs and Challenges

A Young Woman Explores Yosemite, 1915–1917

Laura White Brunner
Edited with an Introduction by Jared N. Champion

 University Press of Kansas

Front matter and notes © 2019 University Press of Kansas

Published by the University Press of Kansas (Lawrence, Kansas 66045), which
was organized by the Kansas Board of Regents and is operated and funded by
Emporia State University, Fort Hays State University, Kansas State University,
Pittsburg State University, the University of Kansas, and Wichita State
University.

Library of Congress Cataloging-in-Publication Data

Names: Brunner, Laura White, 1899–1973, author. | Champion, Jared N., editor
Title: Cliffs and challenges : a young woman explores Yosemite, 1915–1917 /
  Laura White Brunner ; edited with an introduction by Jared N. Champion.
  Description: Lawrence, Kansas : University Press of Kansas, [2019] | Includes
  bibliographical references.
Identifiers: LCCN 2018058814
  ISBN 9780700627974 (cloth : alk. paper)
  ISBN 9780700627981 (pbk. : alk. paper)
  ISBN 9780700627998 (ebook)
Subjects: LCSH: Yosemite National Park (Calif.)—Description and travel. |
  Yosemite National Park (Calif.)—Environmental conditions—History—20th
  century. | Brunner, Laura White, 1899–1973. | Young women—California—
  Yosemite National Park—Biography. | Hikers—California—Yosemite
  National Park—Biography. | Hotel cleaning personnel—California—Yosemite
  National Park—Biography. | Yosemite
National Park (Calif.)—Biography.
Classification: LCC F868.Y6 B835 2019 | DDC 979.4/47—dc23
LC record available at https://lccn.loc.gov/2018058814.

British Library Cataloguing-in-Publication Data is available.

Printed in the United States of America

10 9 8 7 6 5 4 3 2 1

Contents

Editor's Note

Laura White's original manuscript, housed in the Yosemite National Park Archives, is truly something special. The manuscript is typed and organized with the kind of care one might expect from a professional writer. White bound the manuscript exactly the way she hoped the text would be published, complete with a map on the cover, photographs in a center leaf, and other images peppered throughout the text. The map that White included was professionally designed with no clear indicator of who held the copyright, so it is not included in this final version. Similarly, many of the images were also under copyright and could not be included. However, the archives held a number of negatives of photos taken by White herself. I have had these photographs digitally restored for inclusion in the final manuscript. I believe these images add a distinctive and personal touch to the memoir.

As for the text, I took special care to maintain as much of the original prose as possible. The original manuscript exists only in hard copy, so much of my work took place while creating a digital version of the manuscript. When necessary, I changed the language for clarity and precision. White wrote clearly and directly, but the manuscript required some adjustment for conventional punctuation and diction. Her use of commas required significant adjustment to meet contemporary conventions, but the manuscript was otherwise very clean. Overall, it remains largely unchanged, a detail that becomes much more apparent when reading the second section, which was composed primarily of rough-draft material.

I use the introduction to provide some context both for the manuscript itself and for White's significance to environmental history. White kept thorough notes and a number of important artifacts that helped in this process. Despite her thorough and fascinating collection, certain key details remain absent. The records leave many questions about how White began her writing career without a formal education, her moves back and forth across the country, her ascent from working-class laborer to middle-class reporter and memoirist, and her later thoughts on the direction of the National Park Service. Perhaps the most noticeable omission is a more thorough discussion of her friendship with Bill Pontynen. I have scoured the archives and spoken with White's daughter, Alma Brunner Davis, about Pontynen, but these avenues have yielded very little concrete information. Out of respect for the family, White, and Pontynen, I have offered all the details I can confirm about their relationship and have intentionally avoided any speculation.

As the editor, I see my role largely as an intermediary between the archival material and the academic press. I should note as well that this work required the proverbial village. White and her daughter both paved the way for this manuscript through their organization of the materials, to say nothing of their tireless efforts to find a home for its publication. National Park Archivist Paul Rogers and University Press of Kansas acquisition editor Kim Hogeland were both instrumental in ushering this project to publication. Without their guidance, this project might never have come to the surface. Others have helped throughout the process, such as Stan Anderson, who carefully touched up many of the images from photo negatives that were more than a hundred years old. Historians and scholars such as Casey Riley, Anne Mitchell Whisnant, David Whisnant, and Dennis Moore offered invaluable feedback and advice on how to be a responsible steward of the materials. Students Morgan Bradshaw, Thomas Johnson III, and Parker Sewell helped with the more tedious and laborious work required to make such a project happen. Jordin Marron helped sort out the map for the reader's reference. Friends and family, namely Tom and Linda

Jean Jeffrey, Dan and Cynthia Purington, and Zachary Champion, gave me immeasurable support as I traveled back and forth across the country to complete the preliminary research. Finally, this project would not have been possible without the trust and permission of Alma Davis to shepherd her and her mother's hard work across the finish line. For that, I am most grateful.

Introduction

LAURA WHITE BRUNNER

Cliffs and Challenges[1] is the story of Laura White Brunner, Yosemite's most fascinating person whose story has never been told. A woman living at the turn of the century, White had a long career as a journalist, traveled the country for both work and pleasure, and, most significantly, was the second woman ever to climb Yosemite's Half Dome. She lived an extraordinary life marked by adventure and curiosity, yet her legacy has remained buried in the Yosemite archives for nearly thirty years. White[2] was born prematurely on November 7, 1899, and her mother, Eugenia, kept her in the kitchen oven as a makeshift incubator for the first few weeks of her life. Later, White would tell a reporter that she had always wanted to be a national park ranger, but, sadly, she was "born too soon."[3] This phrase, "born too soon," captures her spirit in a number of ways. First, it recognizes the limitations placed on women in that period but recognizes the inherent strength she brought to bear on the challenges she faced. Second, it reveals the optimism with which White viewed the future of women in the park service: she knew that the day would come when women would serve at all levels of the national park system. Lastly, it shows that White approached the world with a sardonic sense of humor and strength that would serve her well throughout her life.

As a teenager, Laura White Brunner spent the summers of 1915 and 1917 working at the famous Camp Curry in the Yosemite Valley. She wrote *Cliffs and Challenges*, the retrospective story

Laura White as a child, c. 1909. Courtesy of Yosemite National Park Archives.

of these summers, some two decades later. Though a teenager working in the valley would usually be unremarkable, White was anything but typical. She had a fiery spirit and never backed down from a challenge. She spent much of her summer working, of course, but she spent her free time climbing the mountains and peaks in the park and renting cameras to photograph her favorite places. Like many working in the park, she hiked throughout the Yosemite Valley, no easy feat considering that most hikes that start at the valley floor require 3,000 to 4,000 feet of climbing before reaching the cliffs' edges.

White first went to Yosemite in 1915 with her mother, Eugenia, following her parents' divorce. Her father was a marble artist, and the family lived on a farm outside Baltimore before moving to San Francisco.[4] Little more is known about her father either before or after the divorce, but White kept significant records of her late teenaged years with her mother. The two made their way to the Yosemite Valley after finding work at Camp Curry thanks in part to a letter of recommendation from Ernest Wilson, a baker and confectioner who had employed them both in Palo Alto in 1914 and described them as "industrious and trustworthy."[5] White was no stranger to labor; she had been taken out of school in sixth grade so that she could find a job.[6] Her working-class background gave her a solid work ethic that served her well as she worked alongside David Curry and his wife, Jennie. The couple had founded the tent village in 1899 as a less expensive alternative to the more luxurious lodges in and around the valley, and Camp Curry was truly the epicenter of much of Yosemite during this formative period. Scholars have credited the Currys with understanding and tapping into a growing middle-class interest in outdoor recreation, as evidenced by the rapid growth in traffic to Camp Curry, especially between 1901 and Laura White's first year there in 1915.[7] Camp Curry represented more than just a new way to visit Yosemite:

White on a cliff, 1915. Courtesy of Yosemite National Park Archives.

it opened up tourism to an entirely new class of Americans. In pairing a private business with the public park, David and Jennie Curry created more affordable lodging as an alternative to the more expensive Sentinel Hotel, thus filling an important role in the park experience for middle-class tourists given that primitive camping had yet to become very popular.

In her memoir, White recounts hard workdays at Camp Curry, where she cleaned hundreds of cabins and made hundreds of beds, each with a specific eye for detail. This detail provides a useful insight into the Currys' view of women's labor as central to the operation of the camp. The Currys demanded a great deal of their staff. A job advertisement read, "A desire to spend the summer in Yosemite is not a sufficient qualification for a position for us—there must also be a desire and ability to perform well your part, whatever that may be."[8] Not surprisingly, the ad leaves women's labor noticeably invisible, but *Cliffs and Challenges* brings forward the efforts made by women at all tiers of the workforce, from White's position as a laborer to Mrs. Curry's role as staff supervisor. As an employee, White had to make sure the rooms were perfectly cleaned and detailed, a truly physical task that required long hours in frigid temperatures. In fact, Camp Curry was located in the coldest corner of the Yosemite Valley because the more expensive hotels, such as the Glacier Point Hotel or Wawona Lodge, occupied the warmer, sunnier spaces. To this day, Camp Curry remains relatively unchanged. The canvas tent cabins still occupy a quiet corner of the Yosemite Valley just below Half Dome.

In the same unapologetically direct tone with which White (not to mention her mother) lived her life, the book recounts many of her hikes and climbs in the Sierra Nevada, including her summit of Half Dome, a trip that would place White in the records as the second woman ever to climb the monolith. Park historian Jim Snyder has claimed that White's climb of Half

Dome was directly responsible for the administration's decision to make the Cables on Half Dome climbing route permanent so that *women* who followed in her footsteps would have a safer path to the top, possibly making the Cables on Half Dome the only sexist trail in existence. The route was first used in 1875 by George C. Anderson, who is thought to be the first American to utilize climbing aids.[9] Interestingly, Ansel Adams would visit the park shortly after White's two summers there, and he would spend six years installing and uninstalling the Cables on Half Dome route at the start and end of each hiking season. The cables that White's hike catalyzed still aid hikers up the back of Half Dome every summer, and the hike is routinely listed among the most dangerous in America.

As American climbers embraced climbing tools such as ropes, pitons, and later carabineers, the masculinized pursuit of independence would be replaced by what climber Charlie Houston would label "the brotherhood of the rope."[10] Mountaineering historian Maurice Isserman argues that broad cultural events such as the Great Depression catalyzed a change in the ways climbers viewed their adventures. He explains that climbing initially reflected a desire for independent manhood, but the focus shifted to a fraternal pursuit "in the shadow of the rapidly deepening Great Depression."[11] While views of climbing shifted broadly from independent to communal, masculinity still remained central to climbing myths and understandings. White's story reflects this tension through photographs that depict her climbing Half Dome alone, with only a handful of photographs showing her alongside her climbing partners. She also walks a careful line between independence and community in her writing, and this balance becomes most precarious when Bill Pontynen, a young man who worked at Camp Curry and who was her regular climbing partner, blames himself for putting the two of them in danger during a particularly trying hike.

Other dangers and adventures litter the memoir, and the book tells of the young White awakening to a rattlesnake atop her sleeping bag during a camping trip, hiking barefoot on Yosemite's granite scrabble because she could not find hiking boots made for women, and refusing to be bound by traditional gender norms. She constantly questioned her mother about matters of propriety, such as why men could not say "legs" in front of women—or perhaps young girls—or why she could not hike alone. Nonetheless, White did hike alone despite her mother's and David Curry's objections. When she was not allowed to wear pants to hike, she pinned her skirts together between her knees as a makeshift solution. In fact, if you look closely at the image of White atop Half Dome's "Nose," you can make out the makeshift pants into which White transformed her skirts to make the ascent slightly less treacherous.

White left Yosemite after the summer of 1917 to work as a "Harvey Girl"—something akin to a flight attendant merged with a housekeeper—on the Santa Fe Railway, where she met her husband, William, who worked as an accident investigator.[12] She visited Yosemite several more times between 1917 and 1922 before settling in William's hometown of Newton, Kansas, where they had two children, Alma (November 9, 1924) and William Jr. (October 12, 1929). Their work meant they were always on the move. Their daughter, Alma, said her father was like a doctor, "always being called out to work."[13] William Sr. suffered serious injuries in a car accident sometime after the birth of his second child and was rendered unable to work, so the family moved to a peach and olive ranch in Rio Linda, California.[14] Here, White became the primary breadwinner for the family and worked six days a week, splitting her time between working in a children's nursery during the day and as a reporter for the *North Sacramento Journal* on nights and weekends.[15] While it is unclear precisely how White managed to secure work as a reporter, given her limited schooling, the fact that she did speaks to the rigor of her self-education and dedication. As a reporter, she never seemed to tire. Alma recalls spending every Sunday on adventures led by her mother, each centered on a trip into nature.[16] Sometimes they went camping or swam in creeks. No matter what, they spent their Sundays outdoors.[17]

White learned her love of nature and travel from her father, who had spent hours teaching groups of children about nature in Baltimore and later in Sutter Woods, when the family moved to San Francisco.[18] Like her father, White never stopped learning, traveling, or reading. She worked, lived, and learned at a breakneck pace, and a newspaper clipping even explains that White's impressive library resulted from this tiresome schedule: because she could not visit the library regularly, White bought as many books as she could so that she could read them on her own time.[19] As one would expect, White passed this independent spirit on to her children: for example, Alma earned her pilot's license in the mid-1950s, a rare feat for a woman of the time.[20]

Nothing about White's life followed a script, from her premature birth and incubation in an oven to her career as a reporter. In many ways, White embraced the world with a wonderfully contrarian attitude. Even the hike up Half Dome was sparked when Bill Pontynen challenged her by saying, "Why, I could break your fool neck the first trip out," in response to which White, not to be dismissed, announced, "I can go anywhere you can go." From then, she notes, "the war was on." White and Pontynen would spend the rest of the summer hiking together, and the two often ended up in dangerous predicaments. White made a terrific hiking partner, and the two remained lifelong friends after their summer in Yosemite drew to a close; White even dedicated *Cliffs and Challenges* to Pontynen, "wherever you are." They stayed in loose contact in the decades after the summer of 1915, and their

White in a tree, 1915. Courtesy of Yosemite National Park Archives.

letters reveal a closeness that never seemed to dissipate over the distance, years, and even White's marriage to a railroad conductor, which might have complicated their friendship.

In January 1943, Pontynen wrote to White from the Las Vegas Army Airfield, which would later become Nellis Air Force Base, where he spent the winter working at a magnesium plant that processed materials to build airplanes for the war. Pontynen was in his midforties at this point and had already served in World War I, so he remained stateside during his service. This was during the early days of the book's creation and White had hoped Pontynen would help her write it, but he declined because he believed she could write it better without him.[21] He was eager to hear from her, though. Early in the letter, he underlined the phrase "still waiting for a line from you" and later asked whether he needed to send along a clamdigger to "pry some words out of you."[22] The two had planned a visit that would have lasted a week and a half, but all resources were dedicated to the war at this point, so Pontynen had no way to travel. He promised to make White a magnesium souvenir as soon as he found the time. He was nostalgic for the days at Mirror Lake, where "you and I sat too often and long to see the moon rise from Tenaya Canyon." He missed White dearly, and in one particularly beautiful passage, he quoted Longfellow before lamenting his own situation: *"Tell me not in mournful numbers, this life is but an empty dream, for the soul that slumbers must be dead and things are not what they seem.* So lonely is this 'Hells Forty Acres' of infernal rock and dust, I'm dying to hear from you, so gather your pen and paper and send me a word of cheer." White replied in the coming months, and Pontynen wrote again in mid-March 1943, apologizing for his directness in asking her to write to him. He again declined the request to coauthor the book, though White jokingly offered him a million dollars for the work.[23] This is the last surviving piece of correspondence between the two.

Cliffs and Challenges: THE FORGOTTEN MEMOIR

White had always been inquisitive and adventurous, often to the frustration of adults around her. She mentions in an autobiographical note that "Laura White Brunner has been writing since she was twelve, when a teacher in a one room school house didn't know what to do with her and gave her a paper and pencil every day and told her to write a story." White would later spend much of her adult life writing for newspapers such as the *Sacramento Bee*, the *North Sacramento Journal*, and her personal favorite, *The Sacramento Union*, as well as a handful of railroad trade magazines following her marriage to William Brunner. She wrote clearly and directly and never lost sight of her passion for the environment. She wrote a great deal for younger audiences—even *Cliffs and Challenges* offers a narrative accessible to a wide range of readers, including young adults—and eventually published snippets from her *Sacramento Union* column on local flora and fauna in a book series titled *Naturettes*.[24] Yosemite has two volumes of these collections in its archives. Sadly, however, one of White's manuscripts, titled *Swinging Doors*, was lost sometime between 1940 and the present day.[25] The manuscript, mentioned briefly in the introduction to one draft of *Cliffs and Challenges*, recounted White's time in the valley from 1917 to 1922.

I began scouting the Yosemite National Park archives. Among the entries, I found one for the Laura White Brunner papers. Almost as an afterthought, an annotation mentioned an unpublished manuscript, and in a flash, I had a project for the foreseeable future. I sent an e-mail to the archivist requesting the first twenty-five pages so I could see whether the manuscript had teeth and received a brief reply some weeks later: "The manuscript is under copyright so I cannot make copies. Bye." After some pushing, the archivist passed along a mailing address for Alma Davis, White's daughter. The contact information gave me very little to work with and, being nearly twenty-five years old, was almost certainly out of date. Nonetheless, I sent a letter to the address and then took to the Internet.

I spent the next eight weeks trying every phone number that appeared to be even remotely tied to Davis's past. I called hundreds of disconnected and wrong numbers, all to no avail. Then, in a desperate effort to keep the project alive, I searched a bootleg Ancestry.com-style website and found a listing for a "possible relative," a man named Ney Davis. Three hours of searching later, I found two obituaries from 1992 that helped me triangulate Ney's connection to Alma. One, from a small, out-of-print paper in California, confirmed that Ney had been married to Alma at the time of his passing in 1992, and the second, from a small town in Pennsylvania, noted that Ney had served on a small Methodist church's finance committee until his last days. I called the church and explained to the administrative assistant that I knew she probably couldn't help, but I had to try. I told her I was looking for a woman who had once been married to a man who had served on the finance committee in the early 1990s, and she cut me off to ask, "You need Alma, don't you? Get a pen."

I was excited, of course, but still worried that my last two months would turn up an empty basket. I called the number and left a message for Davis on her Jitterbug phone—a cell phone specifically designed for the elderly (with huge buttons and an extraloud speaker). I thought that my well had finally run dry, but the next morning, I found three messages waiting on my office phone. Davis had left them, more ready to talk to me with each one.

I called her back immediately, and from the first moment we spoke, I knew that women in this family were a special brand of fiercely independent, no-nonsense people. I told Davis that I was returning her call, and she said simply and directly, "Well, Jared, what do you want?" I told her I wanted to work to publish her mother's manuscript, which I learned during this conversation was titled *Cliffs and Challenges*. I panicked slightly, and instead of asking for copyright permission over the phone, I asked Davis if I could visit her in October during my fall break, to which she agreed. I spent my fall break driving to Pennsylvania to meet Davis, who was living in an assisted care facility just outside Philadelphia. We spoke for a few hours at the kitchen table with the original manuscript in a small box on the table. Davis, wary of my motives, had already spoken to a copyright attorney, who had told her not to let me see the manuscript until she spoke with him following my visit. So there I was, inches from the manuscript that I had spent four months trying to find and still unable to see it. I scribbled a few notes for the attorney, thanked Davis, and went back home to wait.

I planned to drive to Yosemite's archives immediately after giving final exams and made the necessary arrangements with Paul Rogers, the National Park Service (NPS) archivist who managed the collections. The day I was to leave, I finally received a letter from the attorney granting me permission to continue the project, and I was off. White had spent much of her summer working, of course, but she spent her free time climbing mountains and peaks in the park as well as renting cameras to photograph her favorite places, and Yosemite currently holds roughly forty of her negatives along with a few cases of other ephemera.

As one would expect from a professional journalist, *Cliffs and Challenges* affords a predominantly straightforward and clearly written account of White's time in Yosemite. Readers will quickly notice that White emphasizes her frustration with gender norms that restricted her both literally and metaphorically in Camp Curry. However, the narrative complicates our understanding of gender in the national parks by showing Jennie

Curry's authority over the workers, particularly as she sought to shape the working culture and guest experience in the camp. The memoir shows how Mrs. Curry carefully navigated the personalities of her staff and guests and how she played a crucial role in shaping the tourist experience in the early parts of the twentieth century, especially for the growing body of middle-class visitors.

White split the memoir into two sections: the first recounts her most memorable summer in 1915, when she summited Half Dome and climbed a series of other peaks; the second, looking back on the summer of 1917, remains largely unfinished. In the first section, White recalls her many adventures and misadventures as well as her epic climb up Half Dome. She talks about moments of confusion as she sought to understand what it means to be a woman in America and flashes of frustration at the limitations placed on her as a young woman. In the second section, White tells of considerable changes to the Yosemite Valley as well as the working culture at Camp Curry. She looks back nostalgically on her first summer, longs for days with old friends and past adventures, and misses the excitement she felt when first exploring Yosemite. Sadly, the fragments she left make it hard to tell whether she ever managed to reclaim a sense of peace in the valley.

As a writer and journalist, White was meticulous in keeping her photographs and negatives, letters and notes, and all sorts of other materials, all of which were handed over to the Yosemite National Park Archives by Davis following a fifteen-year effort to publish her mother's book. To this day, those archives hold roughly twenty of the negatives and a few cases of other ephemera. Although these materials compose some of the archive's most special holdings, they were initially intended to be read by the public. In fact, White herself spent nearly two decades sending the manuscript to publishers with a brief but powerful cover letter that merely stated, "The stories in this book are all true. I was there."[26] She collected clippings from magazines, newspapers, and other publications regarding the park, especially women in the park. She seemed particularly interested in Enid Michael, the first woman ranger to serve in Yosemite National Park. It seems that White harbored interest in following in Michael's footsteps. In one particularly telling clipping, White underlined the application dates and address for a ranger training seminar.[27]

That the manuscript never made its way into print is nothing short of remarkable, especially because White and her daughter together invested roughly forty years in working to have the book published. Ultimately, the book remained unpublished for several reasons, but the two most significant factors seem to be the limitations of record keeping and publishing about and by women and White's (and later Davis's) attempts to confirm that she had been the first woman to climb Half Dome. Records for women climbers are notoriously poor, and these searches yielded no concrete evidence.

During the early years of the project, White wrote to the Sierra Club in April 1934 to ask whether she had been the first woman to climb Half Dome (it would later turn out that she had not). In his reply, Richard M. Leonard of the Committee on Mountain Records said he suspected that White may have been the first person to summit Yosemite's Cathedral Spires.[28] But after that, the story becomes sticky: Leonard asked for White's photograph to confirm, but there is no record of a reply. It turns out that White had written to Leonard between the 1933 and 1934 climbing seasons, not knowing that Leonard and two of his climbing partners, Jules Eichorn and Bestor Robinson, had failed to summit the peak in 1933 and thus to claim their place in the records as the first summit. When White wrote to Leonard, they were awaiting supplies, specifically pitons, which served as anchors for climbers, to arrive so that they could attempt the summit again in 1934. If White and her friends had truly been to the summit before she wrote to the Sierra Club, then she would have been the first to climb the Cathedral Spires, though it is much more likely that White was among the first to climb Cathedral *Peak*, which would not have required the specialized climbing equipment that she would likely have been unable to afford.

When the Sierra Club lead proved fruitless, White hoped that canisters left atop Half Dome with notes and messages from climbers would contain records to help establish her climb as the first by a woman. She wrote to Wayne W. Bryant, acting chief naturalist of the Department of the Interior, a considerable time later to ask whether these containers were still on Half Dome or perhaps somewhere in the national archives. Bryant replied with a brief note explaining that he had spoken with Mary Tresidder, the wife of former Stanford University president Donald Tresidder and daughter of David and Jennie Curry of Camp Curry fame, who had helped White identify A. C. Pillsbury as the photographer who had captured many of the postcard photographs that she hoped to include in her book. The note suggested the Sierra Club archives as the canisters' possible new home.[29] The canisters never turned up, but White eventually turned her attention to publishing the book regardless of her status as the first woman to summit Half Dome.

She wrote to Charles Carson, a literary consultant, about the book in 1959, specifically to ask about how to handle her mother's divorce and her decision to portray her mother as her sister in the book. Carson said that he believed "the typical mature, intelligent adult . . . would not have the slightest inclination to censure either you or Gene for the way you chose to handle things at the time, when you were both still young and naturally anxious to protect each other from any possibility of disapproval" because "the average adult today has learned to regard divorce as a perfectly normal occurrence. A divorce may be a misfortune, but it is certainly not a scandal." He went on to compare the treatment of divorce to White's discussion of women's hiking clothes as they had been transformed over time. He included some very telling encouragement that revealed some of the isolation White had felt throughout the process: "Don't worry about feeling alone in the writing world. After all, writing is a solitary pursuit, not a group activity. And though you may not find other writers to keep you company right there in your own neighborhood, you can readily appreciate how many there are in the world—struggling writers who sometimes feel just as alone as you feel."[30]

In his first review of the book's draft, Charles Carson noted that White had "given a vivid and lifelike portrayal of yourself as a young girl, convincingly recapturing your own rather naïve and tomboyish feelings of forty years ago. Elsewhere, however, you have taken a more retrospective view, writing as the woman you are today, merely remembering, sometimes rather hazily, the little 'Tops' you used to be." He criticized the description of the landscape as being "fragmentary" to the point that "it is difficult for the reader to develop a comprehensive picture as it would appear to anyone living there or visiting there." He argued that the book seemed rushed, specifically regarding organization and phrasing, and then went on to comment that this very spontaneity was what gave the book its charm. He believed that the order should be reworked to be chronological and that White would need a "change in attitude," specifically in her relationship to the reader. He encouraged her to write from the persona of "Tops," the "fifteen year old 'tomboy'" rather than from the "more mature perspective [she] acquired since this time." He took specific issue with pages 3–4 of the draft, where she apparently spoke in depth about child labor laws and changes to Yosemite, sections she would later omit from the final draft. Later in the letter, he suggested a new outline for the book, which, ironically, replaces White's chronological account with a topically structured piece. He told her to downplay the interpersonal conflicts presented in the first draft because "you are apt to give the reader the idea that you were a disagreeable girl at the time, or that you are a harsh, unforgiving lady today."[31] For Carson and others, gender worked against the manuscript's marketability, an unfortunate underestimation of the text's value and significance.

It appears that White gave up the hope of publishing *Cliffs and Challenges* after her husband, William, died from appendicitis complications in 1960. White herself died on December 22, 1973, from untreated appendicitis. She practiced Christian Science and refused treatment, and Davis regretted that her mother had died of something so treatable. Laura and William are both buried in Arlington National Cemetery, a credit to their service during World War II. The book project sat dormant for nearly another twenty years until Davis took up the task and began working toward publication in the early 1980s. It seems that Davis was also sidetracked by the question of whether White had indeed been the first woman to climb Half Dome, and she gave up the project after a series of family troubles that occurred soon after her discovery that White had been the second woman to summit the monolith. Davis wrote to Marie Byrne of the Bancroft Library at the University of California, Berkeley, to ask whether her mother's Half Dome climb had been the first by a woman, but Byrne replied in January 1984 that there was no record of the climb, due primarily to poor record keeping in the early days of the park.[32] An inquiry to Anna M. Michael of the *Sacramento Bee*[33] and Barbara Lekisch of the Sierra Club yielded similarly fruitless results, though Lekisch went so far as to ask Helen LeConte, wife of the famed explorer Joseph Nisbet LeConte, whether she remembered White or her climb.[34] Lekisch also passed White's story along to Sally Greenwood of *National Geographic* in the hope that it would be useful in the latter's project of writing a history of women mountaineers.

Greenwood wrote to Davis to schedule a visit, but the meeting never materialized.[35] Davis wrote back to Greenwood to say that she had returned to college full time but still wanted to arrange a meeting to discuss the book and other materials. Greenwood believed that the story would fit nicely into a book she was developing with Arlene Blum, perhaps the world's leading historian of women mountaineers.[36] Blum would use much of the research in two books, specifically *Magnificent Mountain Women: Adventures in the Rocky Mountains* (1990) and *Leading Out: Mountaineering Stories of Adventurous Women* (1998). In a letter to Greenwood dated October 9, 1989, Davis reached out again to see whether she could have the book published after so many years. Greenwood had considered including the story in her book on women mountaineers, but life had got in the way for Davis, and the story had been left out. Greenwood had also put Davis in touch with Yosemite historian Shirley Sargent to help sort out the details of the climb and summers in Yosemite. At that point, however, Davis was already discouraged by the process and had resigned herself to merely allowing the story to be a display in the Yosemite library, an idea that Shirley Sargent would eventually reject. Greenwood replied in a handwritten letter some months later—December 29, to be exact—but her work was careless and rushed. Many of the details in the letter were historically inaccurate, such as her claim that White had climbed the Cables on Half Dome route, which had not been installed until four years after White's climb. She also mistook the names of central figures in the story, but the letter was not entirely lacking in usefulness. Greenwood provided Davis with some important context, namely, letting her know that the story would be more likely to find a publisher if Davis could confirm that White had been the first woman to summit Half Dome, a piece of advice that may well have delayed the book's publication for decades.[37]

When Greenwood turned down the project, Davis wrote to Shirley Sargent to see whether the manuscript and other ephemera might make a good installation in the park's museum.[38] Sargent replied that she did not think such an exhibit would have a wide enough audience but that she would like to pass the materials on to park historian Jim Snyder and park librarian Linda Eade.[39] Eade turned down the materials, citing space concerns, but Snyder expressed some interest in having the manuscript published. Davis received a letter from him on February 22, 1990, which was when she learned that her mother's ascent of Half Dome had been by the Clothes-Line rope route that was replaced in 1919 by the iconic Cables on Half Dome route that remains in place today. Snyder also explained that White's climb had been partly responsible for the park administration's decision to install the cables route because of the fear that more women would try to summit the monolith. While Snyder's letter was encouraging regarding the significance of White's climb, he echoed Sargent's belief that there simply was not a place for the materials to be displayed in Yosemite. While he saw the value of the material, he believed that visitors would not be interested in a book with a focus so narrow that it would need to be printed privately, as he believed the market would not support a book about a woman climber. He noted that the Yosemite Association was printing a series for the bookstore in Yosemite but argued that White's book lacked "broad appeal." He thought he might be able to find a home for a few of the photographs and perhaps even excerpts from the book in the Yosemite Association's quarterly magazine; despite his shortsighted undervaluation of the book's market value, he believed it would be an asset in the archives and requested a copy of the materials for research purposes. This letter also helps explain why Sargent never followed up on the book: Snyder wrote a postscript explaining that she was very ill and had even needed to move away from the park so that she could be closer to medical care.[40]

Someone eventually discovered that White was the second, not first, woman to climb Half Dome and wrote "1875" on the back of the photograph of White on the Clothes-Line route, a date indicating Sally Dutcher's ascent with Galen Clark and George Anderson. It is unclear who made this discovery, but what is clear is that White and Davis both gave decades of their lives to the project, eventually turning the materials over to the Yosemite National Park archives. Snyder failed to follow up on the book—his last letter to Davis explained that he would be in the backcountry for a few months but would continue the project when he returned.[41] He never returned to the project, but he added the materials to Yosemite's holdings, where they would sit untouched for nearly twenty-five years.

YOSEMITE, NATIONAL PARKS, AND GENDER IN A TIME OF FLUX

As a housekeeper, White's job at Camp Curry was to make others feel at home, but she never felt quite at home herself, either as a woman climber or as an American in the early 1900s. The memoir recounts a number of moments when she questioned conventional gender norms, never quite managing to understand the logic behind them while still knowing where her boundaries lay. In one example, White compares herself to a guest whom she considers beautiful and concludes that she is "plain" and has no "dazzle." Subtly painful and self-deprecatory moments such as these pepper the story and reveal that White did not quite understand her capacity for adventure and "dazzle" until many years later, when she wrote the manuscript. Nevertheless, her work as a housekeeper in the early 1900s positions her narrative at the crux of gender and feminism during the period. Many scholars have pointed to the gendered rhetoric of housekeeping and homemaking that many Progressive Era women activated to effect change to conservation laws and practices before suffrage. As Carolyn Merchant notes, "Nowhere has women's self-conscious role as protectors of the environment been better exemplified than during the progressive conservation crusade of the early twentieth century."[42] The women of the Progressive conservation movement managed to protect enormous environmental and cultural resources, such as the cliff dwellings in what would eventually become Mesa Verde National Park; the state forest surrounding the Appalachian Trail's northern terminus, Mt. Katahdin; and the Calaveras Big Trees groves just north of Yosemite, to name a few.

While these women managed to shape environmental and conservation policy in tremendous ways that would benefit the nation for more than a century, their work depended on a middle-class ethos that sought to preserve the "separate spheres ideology" that argued that a "true woman's" place was in the literal and metaphorical "home."[43] The separate spheres binary framework for gender relied largely on domesticity as a basis for feminine gender roles: women were understood to be private, nurturing, and morally superior to men, whose placement within the public sphere framed them as rational, competitive, and "naturally" suited to the "rough and violent public world."[44] This framework also helps explain why some women were able to successfully leverage their informal agency to advance prohibition during this period. Collectively, women were able to capitalize on their role as the "moral compass" to steer policy makers to protect the country's natural spaces and resources, a dynamic that becomes even more evident when one considers the way wilderness and domesticity have been linked through offices such as the Department of the *Interior* or terms such as "*domestic* policy."

More recent scholarship has begun to challenge the connections between women, wilderness, and domestic labor. Nancy C. Unger's *Beyond Nature's Housekeepers: American Women in Environmental History*,[45] Polly Welts Kaufman's *The National Parks and the Woman's Voice: A History*,[46] and Stacy Alaimo's "The Undomesticated Nature of Feminism: Mary Austin and the Progressive Women Conservationists"[47] have all made new inroads into rethinking women's roles in environmental and conservation history. Alaimo argues that Mary Austin "saw nature not as a repository of resources for household use, but as an undomesticated, potentially feminist space" that moved outside Progressive Era feminism's "utilitarian conception of nature and promoted women's domestic skills as their qualification for conservation work."[48] In much the same way that Austin's work untethered women from "naturally" domestic womanhood, White described learning to do her domestic labor at Camp Curry without the subtext that this skill came naturally or easily. Her description of work as a housekeeper creates distance from the separate spheres model while still crediting the women laborers in Yosemite with the backbreaking and physically exhausting work that was all too often assumed to come naturally to women of the period.

White's memoir differs from the work of writers such as Austin and Gregory, though, in that White was not doing conservation work per se. Her later work could fit into a narrower definition of conservation writing, particularly her news column "Naturettes." But it makes sense to consider White alongside the likes of Austin and Gregory because *Cliffs and Challenges* was undoubtedly influenced by the themes and motifs of women conservationists. The narrative takes place in the late 1910s, but White wrote the memoir some two decades later, so her near-constant revisions of common tropes for women nature and travel writers appear nothing short of deliberate. Memoir, as a genre, allows for a more careful examination and framing of the past but is subject to the influence of nostalgia. White's work also reflects a long career writing for a young adult audience while maintaining a depth and complexity that speak to all ages.

White's narrative complicates this discourse specifically because she was working class and actually—not just metaphorically—a housekeeper. *Cliffs and Challenges* positions White not as a housekeeper of the land, as many Progressive Era women would have understood her, and her jaunts into the wilderness not as an escape from domestic work, as contemporary notions of gender often frame women's relationship to the wild even today.[49] Instead, her willingness to do housekeeping work affords her the opportunity to explore the Sierra Nevada Mountains surrounding Yosemite.

While her politics remain subtle in *Cliffs and Challenges*, it is clear that White never bought into any concept of "true womanhood" or even the separate spheres model of gender: she scarcely tolerates complaining from women in the backcountry and refuses the notion that her boldness makes her unique or different from other women.

While reading *Cliffs and Challenges*, one should remember that the narrative takes place at a pivotal moment in environmental history, gender dynamics, and American history. Most notably, the success of women's suffrage was imminent, and the NPS was established in 1916, with White's two summers straddling its creation. White's story bridges the complicated narratives of early twentieth-century gender and the environment especially because women played an integral part in early environmental history, culture, and policy even before they were allowed to vote in national elections.[50] For example, women were voting members of the Sierra Club's board of directors since its founding in 1892, and women made enormous contributions to the conversation about public land use. Mary Huston Gregory explored northern California and made recommendations for its governance in her book *Checking the Waste: A Study in Conservation*, and Lydia Adams-Williams, among other women, published pieces with titles such as "A Million Women for Conservation," in which she explains, "Man has been too busy building railroads, constructing ships, engineering great projects, and exploiting vast commercial enterprises to take the time necessary to consider the problems which concern the welfare of the home and the future." Adams-Williams, writing in 1909, spoke to a growing concern among women that industry was harming the domestic space on a national level. In short, women had long served as a check that balanced the male-driven development of lands for profit. This influence would continue in the years to come, and spaces such as Everglades National Park, Biscayne National Park, and Great Sand Dunes National Park would all be protected thanks to the efforts of women and women's groups.[51]

Yosemite, much like the rest of the nation, underwent a massive transition during this period as well. Stephen Mather was named the first director of the NPS in 1916 following a somewhat famous exchange of letters between him and his college acquaintance Franklin Lane, who was serving as secretary of the Department of the Interior. Mather wrote to Lane to complain about the condition of many national parks, to which Lane replied curtly, "Dear Steve, If you don't like the way the parks are being run, come on down to Washington and run them yourself." Lane knew the parks' management needed work and had even said in 1913 that "if the railroads were conducted in the same manner as the national parks, no man would be brave enough to ride from Washington to Baltimore"; thus, he concluded, "the idea of a national park service strikes me favorably."[52]

Mather accepted the offer, but his job went well beyond leading the NPS: in many ways, Mather's job was to define what a national park actually *was*. Could Americans hunt in the parks? Could they build cabins or cut down trees? Were these spaces to develop for profit and industry, as would happen to Yosemite's Hetch Hetchy when it was dammed to build a reservoir to supply water to San Francisco? Were they spaces to conserve for recreational use, as we see now in the Yosemite Valley, or were these spaces to preserve completely, as one might a museum, as we see in modern-day wilderness areas, where use is highly regulated? Would visitors sit by the lakes and simply reflect on nature's beauty, as Frederick Law Olmsted would have wanted, or would they hike and explore the mountains, as John Muir had hoped? These spaces that had once been largely unusable because of poor access were beginning to "open" through technological and infrastructure developments. Prominent Americans turned to Washington to help define the use and value of such spaces, and this outcry would eventually lead to the official creation of the NPS in 1916. Frederick Law Olmsted Jr. had written just four years earlier, "The present situation in regard to the national parks is very bad. . . . They have been created one at a time by acts of Congress which have not defined at all clearly the purposes for which the lands were to be set apart, nor provided any orderly or efficient means of safeguarding the parks."[53] Americans knew the parks were special places but had yet to determine how they would be used. Middle-class tourism was only beginning to become affordable through the advent of automobiles, yet Americans worried about natural spaces being ruined by tourism in the way that Niagara Falls had become a national embarrassment through the overdevelopment of theme park-style attractions that interfered with its natural beauty.[54] Mather would spend much of his tenure as NPS director shaping the ways in which Americans understood and used the national parks.

To do so, Mather embraced emergent transportation technologies, especially automobiles, and he was responsible for Glacier National Park's Going to the Sun Road, the loops through Yellowstone National Park, and—of course—Yosemite's Tioga Pass Road. Mather's goal was to create a "scenic patriotism" through which Americans would, in his words, "See America First,"[55] and so he made access a top priority. As such, Mather entered an arena where "for many years writers, painters, and other artists have played an important role in the representation of various perspectives on the changing nature of the environment for human society and in particular the effect of industrialization and how it should respond."[56] Thus, his decision to improve automobile access to Yosemite and elsewhere marks a significant shift in the way parks would be used. From 1900 to 1901, a few automobiles had been allowed in Yosemite, but they were banned in 1901 because their noise scared horses and disturbed other visitors.[57] Before the initial ban, visitors would pull their vehicles to the edge of Glacier Point for photographs, a practice encouraged by the Glacier Point Hotel management.[58] The ban was lifted in 1913, years before Mather increased access to the national parks through a careful navigation of capitalist demands and conservationist worries by not only allowing automobiles but actually encouraging them. These choices reflect Mather's decision-making process during a period that Alan Trachtenburg terms "the incorporation of America," when industrialization, wage labor, and emergent corporate businesses forced Americans to completely rethink and reconstruct not only their lives but how they viewed the world around them.[59] They also show an impulse similar to the Currys' desire to make the parks accessible to a broader range of Americans. Before the 1920s, most Americans did not own cars, and even fewer could afford train fare to the parks, but Mather recognized the changing economic and technological landscape that allowed greater

access to the parks through automobiles.[60] The Currys also embraced new modes of transportation, albeit for profit motives,
and White's memoir even mentions David Curry's attempt to
secure a permit to bring a train into Yosemite.

White's account bridges this transition, and the narrative's
first section about the summer of 1915 speaks at length about
the difficulty experienced by the housekeeping staff in just arriving in the valley, but these hardships are almost absent during
the second summer that White spent in the valley. In addition,
White recounts the ways in which the Currys sought to shape
how visitors and workers might experience Yosemite. Throughout *Cliffs and Challenges*, White describes how Jennie Curry's
keen eye for detail and hospitality—qualities that earned her the
moniker "Mother Curry" among the staff and guests—coupled
with David Curry's showmanship to create memorable experi-
ences for the guests.[61] While reading about David Curry's boom-
ing welcome to the village, one can easily envision him shouting
to Glacier Point for the "Firefall," a tradition he revived in 1917
of Glacier Point workers shoving embers from a bonfire over
the cliff's edge to create what looked like a waterfall of fire. The
practice was ended decades later, in 1968, when park administra-
tors decided the spectacle was too much like Disneyland.

Yosemite's appeal rests in a delicate, almost paradoxical relationship between tourism and wilderness. While most Americans today draw hard lines between nature and "tourist traps,"
the Yosemite we know today is a product of both tourism and
contemporary notions of wilderness. Historian Jen A. Huntley
points out, "Not only are the two forces [of conservation and
consumer tourism] linked through the nineteenth-century developments at Yosemite, this interconnection is a dynamic and
creative force that changed conservation politics in the twentieth
century and beyond with much of their driving force."[62] James
Mason Hutchings, the original advocate for Yosemite tourism,

was uniquely positioned to spread the word about Yosemite; he partnered with Anton Rosenfield, who owned a publishing house and bookstore in downtown San Francisco.[63] From here, Hutchings could publish maps, guides, and other promotional materials for Yosemite and the surrounding area. San Francisco was the epicenter to a thriving print culture that would later include A. C. Pillsbury, the photographer friend of White who was responsible for many of the postcards sold in the valley during her time. Pillsbury moved his studio to Yosemite after the 1906 San Francisco earthquake, and his hallmark project, a panoramic camera, would benefit landscape photographers in the following century.[64]

Both Hutchings and Pillsbury paved the way for Mather, who also engaged with print media in ways that were new for the parks. In 1921, he published the first *National Parks Portfolio*, which offered Americans the chance to see the parks without leaving home. The goal, of course, was to inspire Americans to visit the national and natural treasures, especially of the West, but the *Portfolio* also indicated the ways that Mather hoped people would engage with the space in the parks. The *Portfolio* project, interestingly, was funded by seventeen western railroads whose leaders hoped to boost travel to the American West.[65] Photographs showed park visitors fishing, hiking, and camping, to name just a few activities, but also depicted men *and* women in the outdoors. The images of women hiking challenged contemporary notions of femininity, even though hiking would have been an acceptable "wholesome" outdoor activity, but the *Portfolio* made sure to temper this challenge by depicting women only hiking with men, being helped by men, or caring for the camp while waiting for men. In short, Mather presented old models of gender in new places with only slight revisions.

White's narrative, particularly in the episodes in which she ventures into the backcountry, sits squarely in this emergent moment before many of the gendered notions about women in the wild were starting to form. Americans were only beginning to explore wilderness as a recreational practice. Thoreau, of course, had wandered about the Massachusetts hillsides almost a century before, but it wasn't until after the Industrial Revolution reshaped the economy that most Americans had money to travel for the sake of travel. The concept of "wilderness" had carried connotations ranging from danger to adventure before this moment, but these meanings shifted as more Americans began to visit the American West just to *see* natural spaces. Eventually, wilderness recreation would come to serve as a site for men to prove their dominance over nature, and for women, wilderness would be seen as at best an escape from domestic tasks.[66]

White's narrative provides a case study before contemporary notions of gender were adapted to the wilderness. Today, scholars have pointed out that advertising and other representations often depict women in the outdoors as either escaping from domestic tasks or in need of male help, but White's memoir depicts her as a capable hiker who uses her work time to create space to hike rather than as something to merely escape, and her need for male help, mainly from Bill Pontynen, are minimal. As such, White belongs in conversations about gender alongside the likes of Isabella Bird and Rose Kingsley. These women, like White, traveled to places such as Yosemite and what would eventually become Rocky Mountain National Park, and Bird would eventually become the first woman to be elected to the Royal Geographical Society.[67] White's narrative is unique in that she was not wealthy or even part of the growing middle class. Instead, she lacked a formal education and performed hard physical labor while in the valley. Bird and Kingsley, while undeniably impressive, had extensive financial resources to fund their travel. Looking back on her time in Yosemite, White recognizes the ways in

White as an adult, c. 1920. Courtesy of Yosemite National Park Archives.

which her working-class status shaped her experience, and the memoir opens with her earning a five-dollar tip that stuns her.

These were incredible years for Yosemite, and White was right in the middle of the valley as the national park and nation both underwent significant changes. John Muir had just passed away, but the Hetch Hetchy dam project that he spent his last days fighting would begin during White's second summer. Cars increased access to the park, and tourists began flooding into the park. Ansel Adams made his first trip to the valley in 1916 and would play a vital role in the ways that Americans understood tourism and art in the American West.[68] Women's groups across America had successfully protected seemingly countless spaces from development, and suffrage was coming to the fore. White's *Cliffs and Challenges* offers a firsthand account of a tumultuous time in American environmental history, and her nuanced and subtle engagement with social issues is nothing short of remarkable, especially in context.

Notes

1. Special thanks to the Yosemite National Park (YNP) Archives and archivist Paul Rogers, who made all of the primary materials available for study.

2. I refer to Laura White Brunner as "White" because she was unmarried during her Yosemite years.

3. Joy Hutchings, "Our Favorite People," date unknown. This article was a newspaper clipping in the YNP Archives, and most of the identifying details were missing. However, the article was written specifically about White.

4. Alma Davis, personal interview with the author, October 11, 2014.

5. Ernest Wilson, recommendation letter to David A. Curry, March 27, 1915, YNP Archives.

6. Laura White Brunner, letter to The MacMillan Company, May 1970, YNP Archives.

7. Peter J. Blodgett, "'The Realm of Wonder': Yosemite and the Business of Tourism, 1855–1916," *California History* 69, no. 2 (1990): 132.

8. Shirley Sargent, "Welllllcome to Camp Curry," *California Historical Quarterly* 53, no. 2 (1974): 137.

9. Maurice Isserman, *Continental Divide: A History of American Mountaineering* (New York: W. W. Norton, 2016), 129.

10. Quoted in Isserman, *Continental Divide*, 162.

11. Isserman, *Continental Divide*, 205.

12. Davis, personal interview.

13. Davis, personal interview.

14. Davis, personal interview.

15. Davis, personal interview.

16. Davis, personal interview.

17. Davis, personal interview.

18. Davis, personal interview.

19. Hutchins, "Our Favorite People."

20. Davis, personal interview.

21. White did manage to write much of the memoir as if Pontynen were a stand-in narrator, especially in the moments surrounding the climbs up difficult peaks.

22. William Pontynen, letter to Laura White Brunner, January 17, 1943, YNP Archives.

23. William Pontynen, letter to Laura White Brunner, March 20, 1943, YNP Archives.

24. E. E. Nichols, letter of support to the publishers of *Naturettes*, December 15, 1948, YNP Archives.

25. White mentions this manuscript in her letter to The MacMillan Company.

26. White, letter to The MacMillan Company.

27. "Yosemite School," magazine clipping, YNP Archives.

28. Richard M. Leonard, letter to Laura White Brunner, April 23, 1934, YNP Archives.

29. Wayne W. Bryant, letter to Laura White Brunner, August 16, 1955.

30. Charles Carson, letter to Laura White Brunner, February 20, 1959, YNP Archives.

31. Carson, letter to Laura White Brunner.

32. Marie Byne, letter to Alma E. Brunner Davis, January 23, 1984, YNP Archives.

33. Anna M. Michael, letter to Alma E. Brunner Davis, January 27, 1984, YNP Archives.

34. Barbara Lekisch, letter to Alma E. Brunner Davis, January 19, 1984, YNP Archives.

35. Sallie Greenwood, letter to Alma E. Brunner Davis, October 9, 1984, YNP Archives.

36. Sallie Greenwood, letter to Alma E. Brunner Davis, August 31, 1984, YNP Archives.

37. Sallie Greenwood, letter to Alma E. Brunner Davis, December 29, 1987, YNP Archives.

38. Alma E. Brunner Davis, letter to Shirley Sargent, August 13, 1989, YNP Archives.

39. Shirley Sargent, letter to Alma E. Brunner Davis, November 9, 1989, YNP Archives.

40. Jim Snyder, letter to Alma E. Brunner Davis, February 22, 1990, YNP Archives.

41. Jim Snyder, letter to Alma E. Brunner Davis, June 1, 1992, YNP Archives.

42. Carolyn Merchant, "Women of the Progressive Conservation Movement: 1900–1916," *Environmental Review* 8, no. 1 (1984): 57.

43. Merchant, "Women of the Progressive Conservation Movement."

44. Paula Baker, "The Domestication of Politics: Women and American Political Society, 1780–1920," *American Historical Review* 89, no. 3 (1984): 620.

45. Nancy C. Unger, *Beyond Nature's Housekeepers: American Women in Environmental History* (Oxford, UK: Oxford University Press, 2012).

46. Polly Welts Kaufman, *National Parks and the Woman's Voice: A History* (Albuquerque: University of New Mexico Press, 2006).

47. Stacy Alaimo, "The Undomesticated Nature of Feminism: Mary Austin and the Progressive Women Conservationists," *Studies in American Fiction* 26, no. 1 (1998): 73–96.

48. Alaimo, "The Undomesticated Nature of Feminism," 73.

49. Jamie N. McNiel, Deborah A. Harris, and Kristi M. Fondren, "Women and the Wild: Gender Socialization in Wilderness Recreation Advertising," *Gender Issues* 29 (2012): 39–55, doi: 10.1007/s12147-012-9111-1.

50. A good starting point for scholars interested in questions of gender and environment is the essay collection *Seeing Nature through Gender*, edited by Virginia Scharff (Lawrence: University Press of Kansas, 2003).

51. For more on women's influence on national park development, see Kaufman, *National Parks and the Woman's Voice*.

52. "Preface," *National Park Service: The First 75 Years*, edited by William H. Sontag (Eastern National Park and Monument Association, 1990), https://www.nps.gov/parkhistory/online_books/sontag/sontagoa.htm.

53. "The Olmsteds and the Development of the National Park System," *The Master List of Design Projects of the Olmsted Firm 1857–1979* (Washington, DC: National Association for Olmsted Parks and National Park Service, 2008), http://www.olmsted.org/the-olmsted-legacy/the-olmsted-firm/the-olmsteds-and-the-development-of-the-national-park-system.

54. Alfred Runte, *National Parks: The American Experience*, 4th ed. (Lanham, MD: Taylor Trade, 2010), 1–9.

55. Runte, *National Parks*, 75–94.

56. Stephen L. Wearing, Matthew McDonald, Jo Ankor, and Stephen Schweinsberg, "The Nature of Aesthetics: How Consumer Culture Has Changed Our National Parks," *Tourism Review International* 19, no. 4 (2015): 227.

57. Paul C. Johnson and Lewis C. Laylin, "Turn of the Wheel: The Motor Car Vs. Yosemite," *California Historical Quarterly* 51, no. 3 (1972): 205.

58. Johnson and Laylin, "Turn of the Wheel," 207.

59. Alan Trachtenburg, *The Incorporation of America: Culture and Society in the Gilded Age* (New York: Farrar, Straus and Giroux, 1982).

60. Hal K. Rothman, *Devil's Bargains: Tourism in the Twentieth-Century American West* (Lawrence: University Press of Kansas, 1998), 144.

61. Sargent, "Welllllcome to Camp Curry," 132.

62. Jen A. Huntley, *The Making of Yosemite: James Mason Hutchings and the Origins of America's Most Popular National Park* (Lawrence: University Press of Kansas, 2011), 3.

63. Huntley, *The Making of Yosemite*, 66.

64. Amy Scott, ed., *Yosemite: Art of an American Icon* (Berkeley: University of California Press, 2006), 205.

65. Barry Mackintosh, "Parks and People: Preserving Our Past for the Future," in *National Park Service: The First 75 Years*, ed. William H. Sontag (Eastern National Park and Monument Association, 1990), https://www.nps.gov/parkhistory/online_books/sontag/sontag3.htm.

66. Jamie N. McNiel, Deborah A. Harris, and Kristi M. Fondren, "Women and the Wild: Gender Socialization in Wilderness Recreation Advertising," *Gender Issues* 29 (2012): 48–49, doi: 10.1007/s12147-012-9111-1.

67. Karen M. Morin, "Peak Practices: Englishwomen's 'Heroic' Adventures in the Nineteenth-Century American West," *Annals of the Association of American Geographers* 89, no. 3 (1999): 511.

68. Jonathan Spaulding, "Yosemite and Ansel Adams: Art, Commerce, and Western Tourism," *Pacific Historical Review* 65, no. 4 (1996): 615–639.

Cliffs and Challenges

By

Laura White Brunner

A Story of Yosemite
1915 and 1917

Dedicated to
Bill Pontynen,
wherever you are

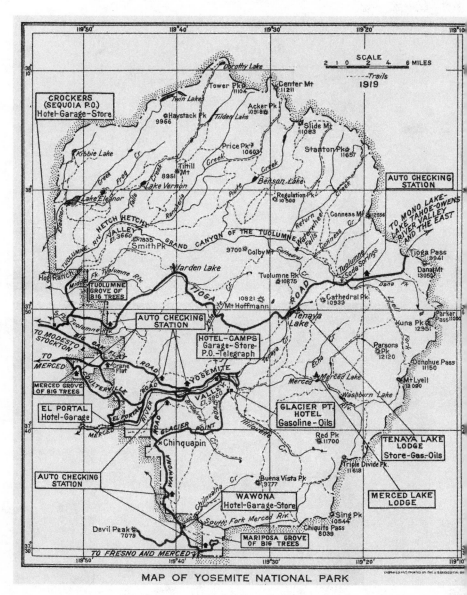

MAP OF YOSEMITE NATIONAL PARK

General Information Regarding Yosemite National Park. Washington, DC: Government Publishing Office, 1919. Courtesy of Yosemite National Park Archives.

Yosemite
1915

"Madam, our help are the sons and daughters of my friends; I know who they are; I don't know who you are." Mr. Curry was using his stentorian voice and he cut each word sharply.

"If mixing with my help annoys you?" he continued.

"It does," she interrupted him. She tried to stretch another inch to prove she was not afraid of this huge man before her and glared with all the ferocity she could bring into her small black eyes.

"I repeat, madam, if it annoys you, and you say that it does, I will have my head porter, who by the way is one of Stanford's finest students, get your suitcases and take you to the Yosemite Falls Camp. They maintain a strict division of guests and help there."

He had put special emphasis on the last word, and the madam stalked away with her head in the air.

I peeked from behind a tent and pantomimed a big clapping.

He wiggled the stub of his index finger at me, twisted his mustache, and strode on, calling greetings and good mornings.

"Get your aching backs out of bed and to breakfast before the cook gets hot and burns the bacon—Did you make it to the point, or did you eat too much of my good grub and could puff up the grade?—Come now—up everybody—the birds have been up for hours—the falls are roaring for your attention, come—up—up—up."

I knew that his eyes were dancing. His hands were waving

to guests and help alike as they poured out of their tents and dashed to washrooms. The spirit of the camp was getting a good start. Someone was bursting into a song and someone else was joining in. Help or guest, it didn't matter. He loved them all and they loved him. Unless, of course, it was someone like the disgruntled old dame.

I had been witness to the little fracas because one of my "tenters," Madam Alexander, the opera singer, had asked me to come see her before breakfast.

I reached her tent and called her name.

"Come in, my dear," and she motioned for me to sit down on the bed. She was so beautiful that even the tent had a glow with her presence and perfumes. The top of the dresser was covered with jewelry and small bottles, that must have had something to do with the difference. I had never had a drop of perfume on me, but the beautiful bottles were a joy to look at.

"Please, Miss Alexander, don't leave your jewelry out in the open; the pack rats are something awful. I put everything in the drawer yesterday and left you a note."

"Yes, I know you did, and that is why I want to talk to you."

"Oh," I gasped, thinking that she had missed something and was blaming me. My face must have registered my feelings and she quickly quieted my fears.

"No, it's not that, my dear—I've watched you closely this week, ever since the day you found me lying here with that dreadful headache and helped me into bed and went and got something to relieve the pain. The nice way you had of caring for me, I liked it." She raised herself on her pillow and reached for my hand. "I need you. When I leave here tomorrow, I am going to Europe, on tour, by way of San Francisco, and by ocean liner via the Panama Canal. I'd like to have you for my personal maid."

"What would I have to do?" I finally stammered.

"Oh, just be sweet and nice to me as you have been this week, hang up my clothes, run my bath, oh, a thousand things I don't have time for. Maybe sew a button or mend a tear in a blouse."

My thoughts were going round and round. Gene would never let me go in the first place. I'd have to grab at some excuse, and when she said what she did about sewing, I spoke right up: "I'd ruin everything you have." It wasn't exactly so, but I couldn't see myself sitting all day sewing laces and silks, even if it meant Europe.

"I'm sorry," she said and pressed a five-dollar bill into my hand.

On my way back through the camp, I ran into Mr. Curry again. He put his arm over my shoulder and said, "Are you going with her?"

"How did you know?" I blurted out.

"The lady and I had quite a talk last night after supper. If I would let you go without any trouble. Why didn't you want to go—or are you going?"

I pulled away from him as though insulted and asked, "Go where? Leave the Valley?—Why, Mr. Curry?"

"That's the girl!" And he sure laughed heartily. The guests began to gather around. "That's the way I like to hear you talk. Remind me to put another dollar in your pay envelope. You better run along to breakfast or you won't get any bacon."

That made everybody laugh and I left them joking and teasing each other about their aching bones and blistered feet.

A dollar indeed, in a pay envelope I would never see because Gene would use the money for our bills, but as she said, "You get your meals and a place to sleep and your tips, what more do you want?"

Tips were usually two bits, or even a dime and once in a while a fifty-cent piece. Here I was with a five-dollar bill, the biggest tip I could ever expect to get. Well, I would get a pair of tennis shoes I needed, rent a camera and take some pictures of my own, and I would put the rest of the money in my special hiding place.

I glanced back at this man who was loved and known by millions, kings and queens, presidents and lawmakers, poor men and rich men. All had thrilled to his "Welcome" and his joking and his mile-high call to Glacier Point, to the Fire Fall,[1] "Let her go!" and his "Farewell."

I had seen Mr. Curry for the first time over three months before. To be exact, it was Saturday, April 15th, 1915, on the platform at the Palo Alto railroad station, the Stanford University town, south of San Francisco, California.

We had just checked our trunk and were struggling with our heavy suitcases. A big man separated himself from one of the groups and approached us and asked, "Going to the Valley?"

Gene set her suitcase down and shook his hand and said that we were, and that we had just checked our trunk. She introduced me, and he turned and smiled. That more than surprised me. I usually received a cold stare, an annoyed frown or grim silence.

He called out to the group of men, "George,—Hal," and motioning to the suitcases said, "See that these get up to my office, no, I mean El Portal, tonight, forgot we have to stay over. But I'll have my own train before the summer is out. Just you wait and see." A great "Hurrah" went up from the group as he rejoined them, calling back to us, "See you girls later."

"Great guy," said one of the men as he relieved me of the suitcase. "Come on over and meet some of the others. We're going to be sharing the same camp; might as well get to know us."

He smiled at Gene, and did she love it! Her cheeks flushed

---

1. The Fire Fall was a controversial practice in which workers at Glacier Point would dump the hot embers from the nightly campfires over the edge of the cliff at Mr. Curry's command from the valley below. The practice ended in 1968.

pink, and she smiled back. Sometimes I was sure I could hear her purr.

The train came in and we all scrambled aboard. I didn't know where we were going. Gene had said we were going to Yosemite, and I had asked if there were palm trees there, and she had said "yes" and told me to wash behind my ears. I often wondered why, for nobody had looked behind them yet. She probably hadn't heard me and said "yes" just out of habit.

I had noticed several boxes packed, and that always meant we would be on the move again. More nice books left in a school for someone else to read. This business of kids being seen and not heard was getting tiresome.

Different ones came to our seat and made themselves known and stayed and chattered awhile. One of them turned the seat in front of us around so that it faced us and two could sit down and sometimes a couple stood in the aisle. Names began to be associated with faces and they answered Gene's questions.

"How did the Currys get started?" was one of them.

One of the older men had a clipping from a paper, with a picture that showed the first Camp Curry in 1899. Gene looked at the picture, and looked my way and raised her eyebrows and grinned. She didn't have to say what she was thinking. The one word 1899 and "Um—" had said plenty. That was the year I was born, and I was supposed to be eighteen, but I wondered whom I was fooling. Long skirts to my ankles and my hair on top of my head may have helped, but eighteen was a long way off as far as I was concerned.

I leaned over to look at the picture. I could recognize Mrs. Curry by her smile; the other women in their tight, high-necked, long-sleeved long dresses looked sad and tired and uncomfortable.

The man Jedidiah said that he had been with them almost from the beginning, and that the Currys had met while going to the University at Indiana. After they were married, they had taught school for a while, even though Mr. Curry had studied for the ministry.

"A minister!" said the other men, and whistled. "Why don't somebody tell a guy these things. If he is helping the man upstairs to keep the books, I'd better watch my language this summer."

"I guess he has been watching your heart and not your tongue," put in Gene with her prettiest smile. Well, that endeared her to them right there.

"Oh, I'm not sure you got a heart, but you said you were like one of the family, so I don't think you have to worry. You said you have been keeping the campfire going for fifteen years," spoke up the man with deep wrinkles, named James.

"Yep, I came in with them," continued Jedidiah. "Horses and wagons, seven tents, and three children. Took us three days from Redwood City, where he was principal of the high school. It was vacation time and we came to Stockton on a river boat, and then on to Coulterville."

He sighed, "Yep, I couldn't read nor write, but I kept 292 guests warm that first summer I was with them. Now we got 500 tents, and they tell me we're goin' to put up 500 more this next month. I guess that is why they hired your strong back, young fellow."

"You're right for once," answered Hal. "And the kid is going to feed the squirrels."

"You're wrong," said George, "she's going up to help butcher the deer the Indians bring in."

Before we had reached the end of the line at El Portal, we had heard so much that might be true and so much that had been stretched for the effect, and we had laughed so much with the rest of them, I realized they had outdone themselves to make us welcome.

The train that had wound in and out and jerked back and forth on the tracks finally came to the end of the line. Soot and cinders had come in the open window and all of us had dark circles around our eyes and cinders in our hair, and someone said they were beginning to feel gritty. I was beginning to wonder if I could stand up and walk straight.

I said something to Gene about the soot and she said that "nobody expected to be comfortable when traveling."

By sundown the windows had been pulled down because it began to get colder. As we stepped off the train, I laughed to see everyone steaming. Then I realized that the mist going by the end of my nose was the same thing. I heard someone say it was frost. Whatever it was, I was cold. Palm trees indeed; why, Gene hadn't even heard me talking to her. She seldom did. When I asked her why I couldn't have worn my big "rough-necked" sweater instead of my thin coat, she said my coat and hat were proper.

Once in the lobby and standing beside the big open fireplace, it was better. We watched the men unload all the baggage and bring in the suitcases. We just waited to be told what to do next.

Mrs. Curry, who was at the hotel, came up and told us our room number, and went with us to show us the dining room. "Go up now to your room and freshen up a bit and I'll meet you here in an hour." She smiled and was gone.

I had served Mrs. Curry ice cream and candy orders in the candy store, where I sometimes worked after school and on weekends, and Gene had no doubt talked to her in the adjoining bakery. She had asked Gene to go up to the Valley and help set up camp. At least that is what I heard Gene tell someone on the train.

I didn't know that I would be joining thousands of other people who called her Mother Curry. I had never called anyone mother. Gene felt her responsibility (at times) as a parent, and had given me strict orders not to call her mother; said it made her feel old. So I had gotten in the habit of calling her Gene and hearing her referred to as my sister, until it almost seemed as though that was the way of it. At least she said it was more mod-

Camp Curry, 1915. Photo by Laura White, courtesy of Yosemite National Park Archives.

ern, whatever that was. I guess it had something to do with the new freedoms for women.

We always had a rumor, and at night when these so-called girls had their hair down and brushing, I would hear them talking. I guess the divorce business was also more modern. Anyway, I liked it better when Papa was home and we were a family. And a new thing was coming up, called the vote, and women were going around the country with little hatchets and breaking beer bottles. I couldn't see where that solved anything, but I was told I would understand someday.

As I found out later, Mr. Curry greeted the guests, answered their questions, pointed out the points of interest. In fact, he used to say that was the way he lost his finger, "Just plain wore off."

He woke the guests in the morning with his stentorian voice, joked, and kept up the morale of the camp. It was Mrs. Curry in her more quiet way that saw that the hurt and injured were cared for, settled disputes, and kept an eye on the supplies and the kitchen.

Her daughters, Mary and Marjory, came up later when college was out. Mary started dating Don Tresidder and they were married in 1920. He was studying medicine at Stanford. Marjory also married a Stanford man, a Bob Williams. Foster, the Curry son, and his wife and baby were also part of the camp. I knew them only by sight. By the time the two girls arrived, I was up to my ears in so much excitement that I wasn't aware that many of the college kids had groups of their own.

I was so involved with the crazy things that were happening close around me, and I knew most of the workers by whatever name they were called (first or last or nickname or for real); most of them called me "the kid," being the youngest. They were spoiling me so much that otherwise I never would have had the nerve to challenge Bill's ability as a hiker, but more of that later.

Back to El Portal, that cold evening. Gene and I climbed the stairs to the room assigned to us. I curled up on the bed with a blanket over my shoulders and watched her and wondered why we were so different.

She had beautiful hair, curly and soft and shiny brown. She did it up in little ringlets around the back of her head. She had told me once that for a ball given in her honor at the Saint Francis Hotel, in the "good old days," she had a hairdresser style her hair, and the curls were pinned around a long strand of sky-blue tiny shells that Papa had bought her from Hawaii. The hairdresser had used 500 invisible hair pins. I could remember that night, how beautiful she was dancing with the long folds of the Chinese silk formal that changed color as she whirled around. She was the "Belle of the Ball." She was twenty-six at the time and she was told she looked only twenty, just as today people told her at thirty-five that she didn't look a day over twenty-five. She loved the flattery, but I was sure she was harder to please and she lost her temper more often. It must be hard for pretty people to grow older.

Now as for me, at fifteen, nobody paid any attention to a plain person that had no dazzle. If I complained, Gene would say I was feeling sorry for myself and my turn would come someday. What most of the silly, good-looking girls were always giggling about didn't look funny to me. I'd tell them they could have their joy-rides and rag-time, and they would call me sour-grapes, and say that no boy would have any time for a tomboyish girl with her nose in a book all the time. Well, I could kick a football as far as any boy and I never missed the basket in basketball, and I could outrun any of them that were in my school. So I let these so-called girls tease me if they wanted to.

While I was rambling, Gene had her hair fixed, and her glasses perched on her very straight nose. They gave her an air of distinction, somebody had said. When she walked or rather glided around, people just had to turn and look. Her hands were different, they never looked like working hands. Her clothes always looked pressed and brand new even when they were years old. Well, she brought me up quick, as she finished adjusting her lace collar.

"You better get moving, if you want to make a decent appearance. Be sure that your petticoats are not showing. I'll wait for you in the lobby." And with that she glided through the door and left me to try and do something with myself.

I rolled myself off the bed. What was the use? Even after I had washed, I couldn't see any difference, not even in my hair after I had struggled with the brush. It was still dull and blew helter-skelter. I hated mirrors; I always got along better when I didn't look into them. My snub nose and big teeth looked just the same, but I went through the motions of cleaning up, and hitching up my three petticoats and trying to smooth out the wrinkles in my skirt. I shouldn't have curled up on the bed.

I took another look in the mirror and saw that part of my pug was loose again. I just couldn't make the hairpins hold in the right places. There ought to be a way to pin the things into your head. I finally gave up and dashed out of the room and down the stairs to the lobby, only to catch Gene's eyes and a shake of the head. "Can't you come down the stairs like a lady?" she said when I got up to her.

She was sure feeling her responsibility today. Most of the time she was fun.

Mrs. Curry was coming down the stairs as a lady should, and she came over to us all smiles, and said how rested we looked; and after a few nice greetings to different ones in the lobby she led the way into the dining room.

I don't remember a thing we ate, but I do remember the things Mr. Curry talked about and the little interesting things Mrs. Curry brought into the conversation. Even Gene told how she had come to the Valley in 1903 with my Papa's Uncle and family. They came in by horse and wagon, camping on the way.

Mrs. Curry remembered him, especially because of his long, flowing white beard. "I remember him well. His camp was in the meadow between our camp and the Arches. They came up every summer with their two boys and their friends. His beard reached to his waist. He kept it divided and braided and tucked into his vest pockets on week days when working, but on Sundays when he joined us for worship services, that beard, beautifully shiny and rippling in waves, just covered his starched white shirt. It always reminded me of Vernal Falls with the sunlight on it."

Mr. Curry laughed so heartily that everyone in the dining room looked up and smiled. They were happy with him even though they didn't know what the joke was.

One of the older men leaned over to me and said, "You see, when the Stentor laughs, it makes the whole world happier."

Mr. Curry settled back into his chair thoughtfully and then turning to Gene asked, "Wasn't there a rattler in your bed that year?" I could hear an intake of breath by several. Then he continued, "Some of my campers wanted to go home, and that is why I remember it so well, I had quite a time convincing them that if they kept up their usual noises and kept tramping around, the snakes would not come anywhere near the camp. I told them that you folks were alone in the big meadow, and slept on the ground, that you were no doubt sedate, quiet folks, and the night had been unusually cold, and the snake was just looking for a place to sleep."

"The snake was not exactly under the covers," Gene answered. "You see we were sleeping in a row bed. Four mattresses had been laid side by side, and a set of covers would cover four of us. Aunty was next to me on the left, with Uncle on the outside, with the shotgun beside him. He used it only to scare away the mountain lions that made the horses restless, and there was a big dishpan and iron spoon handy to scare away the bears.

"Laura was next to me on my right. The next two mattresses held the two boys and their friends. I believe Manley, the oldest, was on the outside with the same equipment beside him.

"A snake hadn't been seen for years, and we never mentioned them, and if we had been worried, we would have strung a hair rope around the bed, for in those days everyone believed that a snake would not crawl over one."[2]

2. Many believe that placing a rope around a sleeping bag will prevent snakes from crossing to be near a person, but this is generally understood to be closer to superstition than fact.

All eyes at the table were on Gene and she loved it. Besides, all mountain people loved stories, especially if they are true ones. Next to bears, a snake story is best to get complete attention. No one wanted to lose a word.

While everyone was drooling with suspense, Gene side-tracked to tell why she liked to wake up early and listen to the bird noises, and watch the occasional deer slipping through the trees, and hear the snort of the horses, and especially, she glanced over at Mr. Curry with one of her sweetest smiles, "Listen to the Stentor waking up his camp."

She was a born actress and knew just about how much suspense her audience could stand before snapping their buttons off. Everybody sighed and caught the extra breath he needed but no one made a real sound; that would have spoiled the story, and they instinctively knew it.

She continued, "I turned my head toward Half Dome, where the sun was just coming around the side, and then ahead to get a good look at Glacier Point in its morning glory." She sighed, and I knew that she was going to give her punch line.

"It is a good thing that at times I can control my impulse to scream, for when I glanced down to see if Laura was covered," and she looked around to see that no one's attention had wandered, "well, there was a rattler,—curled right up on top of her, not six inches from her face."

Someone slowly whispered, "What did you do?"

"I wanted to scream, but of course I must have known that would have been fatal,—I turned my head and in a whisper called, 'Uncle—Uncle—help me! Don't move, but tell me what to do if you hear me.'

"Uncle Joe answered back, 'What's the matter, Gene?'

"'There's a rattler curled up on top of Laura.'

"'Hold still, all of you,' he whispered back, for he must have known that all of us were awake by then. 'One move from any one and it could cost the baby's life.'

"I could hear the faintest rustle as he inched out of the bed, and from the corner of my eye I could see him roll about five feet away before he stood up and then he circled around in back of us to where Manley was.

"He returned to his side of the bed, and Manley had crept up slightly behind our heads. Uncle must have given a signal, for quicker than I can tell it, that top cover was grabbed upwards and rolled to the foot of the bed."

Everyone exhaled, and Gene relaxed in her chair before she continued.

"I just can't describe the next few minutes. Everyone jumped out of bed, and the hollowing was awful and I saw people rushing from your camp, and I wanted to scream but I couldn't and the last thing I remember was when Uncle Joe shot the gun. I passed out. When I came to, several women were bending over me, and Auntie was bathing my face with water."

"What was Laura doing?" someone asked.

"Do what she always does," said Gene. "Scare me to death, and then go on sleeping, or just go to sleep as though nothing had happened."

After that they changed the subject and talked about the railroad. One of the other guests had come over to the table and asked Mr. Curry when he was going to get his permit from the Interstate Commons to have a train of his own. Mr. Curry got up and went with him to the lobby to talk man-talk. Someone else asked Mrs. Curry the same question.

"Yes, we are trying to get a special train of our own, so our guests can come right into the Valley the same day they leave and not have to stay overnight, here at the hotel."

"Are they extending the railroad?" someone asked.

"No, we are only asking that the schedule be set for an earlier start from Los Angeles and San Francisco, so that they will arrive here in the late afternoon instead of the evening. In that way we can have our buses meet the train, and have them in camp in time for a late supper or rather a second serving of a supper we will plan for them."

"Are the horse-drawn stages being taken off the roads entirely?" one of the men asked.

"Yes, now that the motor cars are to be used. It would be too dangerous for both modes of travel."

"I am going to miss the thrill of watching the old freight wagons pulling into the Village," spoke up the man called Jedidiah. "In the first place, I still think letting a slow, cautious mule or horse pick his way into the Valley gives a body a chance to look around and absorb what you're seeing—I don't see what all this need for hurrying is for, anyhow. If you'll excuse me, Mother Curry. I'm not much for dessert anyway. Think I'll go talk to some of the ol' timers a bit."

Mrs. Curry watched him leave the dining room, then she turned to us and said, "Good old Jedidiah, the new ways and progress annoy him. He drove our supply wagons for years, and never complained about the hardships or breakdowns. When we came in on the newly completed railroad in 1907, he accused me of treating him like an old man. Now, of course, since he will not learn to drive, I will have to insist that he find something else to do in camp. We have disposed of our horses and rent horses from the barns for the few weeks needed to set up camp. He may consent to take charge of the horses. More people will come to the Valley if they can make the trip quickly. So we will have to accept the changes."

We left the table after our dessert had been served and spent the rest of the evening in the lobby, with more talk of the railroad and horses. Some thought that being the first to go in by bus would be a great thrill. I was sure that I would have preferred the horse stage instead. I had only been in a car a few times and had not enjoyed it at all. It was spit and sputter and smelly and jerky. So, like Jedidiah, I was sure I would have preferred the horse-drawn wagon.

Another thing that they talked about was the weather. It was plenty nippy where we were, but they all assured me that the Valley was much colder. It was reported that the snow was practically gone from the floor of the Valley but that there was plenty on the rim. I think that someone said that the floor of the Valley was 4,000 feet, and the rim was three or more thousand feet higher.

I was assured that when I went to bed in a tent, just twenty miles from a glacier, I'd know it. "You put your clothes in bed with you, between the blankets," one of the men volunteered, "otherwise you will wake up in the morning and find them frozen. Once you have to crawl into ice-coated pants, you'll remember."

Gene flushed a deep pink and the man said, "Sorry miss," and walked away.

Just then Mrs. Curry came over and reminded us that we would be called early, for breakfast was at seven and we would leave for the Valley by eight. We said good night and climbed the stairs to our room.

Soon as we were in the room, I asked Gene what the man had said "Sorry miss" for.

She straightened up another inch and looked down her nose at me as she did when she remembered that I needed training. "A gentleman does not mention some things in front of a lady. Pants, indeed. Why, your Father had never seen my ankle before we were married, and he never would have used the word 'legs.'"

"What in the world did he think held you up?" I asked. "And what are you supposed to call them?" I ducked a backhanded slap, but I was laughing inside.

"Don't you dare be flip with me, young lady," she warned me.

I sat on the bed as she unsnapped the suitcases and took out two light cotton gowns. "Why didn't we wear the long underwear you said you brought?" I thought of the two long, soft flannel gowns I had seen in the chair the night before.

"I knew it would be cold in the Valley this time of year but I certainly didn't expect it to be so cold here," she answered. "The sooner you get into bed the quicker you will get warm."

I wasn't long getting into bed, where I watched her in her precise preparations for the night. Her waist was hung carefully on a hanger and put in the closet, and her skirt was folded and placed under the mattress at the foot of the bed to keep in the crease. Her three petticoats, one flannel and short; the cotton and plain a few inches longer; and one nainsook with tucks and lace, two inches longer, were shaken well and hung in the closet. Her corset-cover was inspected for any tears in the lace and laid carefully over the chair. Then she slipped her gown over her head to finish undressing as a lady should. One of our renters had a gown you could see through. It seemed silly to wear a gown that didn't cover you up.

I went on watching Gene. Her gathered bloomers fell to the floor. I could tell from the workings of her arms that she was unhooking her corset, then it fell to the floor. I was watching for the undershirt to come next but she thrust her arms into the sleeves of the gown.

"You always take off your shirt," I said, surprised that she would break her routine.

"It's cold, so I decided to leave it on," and then she giggled, "You did," and she glanced over to the chair where my things were all bunched up. "You are a bad influence for me. I have to be careful or I will be disrobing like an alley-cat, too."

I knew that she was only spoofing me but just the same I wasn't an alley-cat, but I grinned back at her.

She picked up the corset and loosened the strings and hung it over the foot of the bed (to let out perspiration). I had been called down many times for saying "sweat." "A lady does not sweat," she had reminded me.

She next picked up the bloomers and shook them, commenting, "I don't like these new bloomers at all; the split panties are cooler; but I thought that we would be climbing around and these would be more practical. When we get back to civilization, I am going to make up some of those Teddy-Bears. One of the girls at the bakery had a pair and they looked real nice."

Not having seen any I said, "Sounds like they belong in the mountains."

"Silly, you can't go by names, these days. They are a sort of combination of corset-cover and loose panties with a strap between, and lots of lace and ribbons. Real pretty, and expensive to buy, but I could get some nainsook and lace at the five and dime, and make up some for next summer, real cheap." Then she sat down on the side of the bed and got that dreamy look in her eyes that she always got when she talked about clothes.

One arm hung down over the brass rail of the bed, at the foot, and she went on as though talking to herself. "The stores are featuring the real latest Chinese silk in color, a real pretty pink—but old Granny Thompson, the dressmaker, said that pink panties, lipstick and rouge aren't decent."

She sat up and went to the dresser and began to take the pins out of her hair. She stood jabbering about clothes until she was sure she had brushed fifty times.

Then she put the bloomers and the corset-cover and the corset in the closet and laid out her serge robe across the foot of the bed with her bed slippers below on the floor, looked out of the window and debated opening it, decided against it, pulled up the shade "in case of fire" and told me for the thousandth time how someone had burned up because the shade was down and the flames weren't seen. Then she tested the key in the lock and slid the chair under the knob. Last, as always, she went to her purse in the bureau and took out a small can of red pepper, slid the lip back a little and set it on the stand beside the bed. "Just in case someone did get in, belt pins are well enough for daytime use and when you are awake, but hard to find in your sleep or when half awake."

I asked her if red pepper wasn't hard to find, too, to which she replied that "one whiff would wake you up, and a woman could always scream."

"I think all those men going to the mountains seem awfully nice. I didn't see one of them that I would want to stick a pin in. I don't see why I would want to anyway."

"You hang on to your big pin for now. When you are older I'll tell you some more tricks." And she pulled the blankets up around her ears, her sign to tell me to stop talking.

Well, Gene was interesting even when she sounded silly. I thought of the play she had taken me to—*Dr. Jekyll, Mr. Hyde*—the man who was thinking of being bad always had a green light around him first, so all I had to worry about was watching them starting to turn green, so I turned my back to her and went to sleep.

Morning was announced by a knock on the door by the bell-boy. Of course, Gene bounced out of bed as one should. I knew from the sound that she had poured some water into the basin on the wash stand and would be washed and dried in no time at all. She was partly dressed and finished with her hair before she got cross enough with me to really make me move. Even said she had called me three times. Of course, she hadn't but there again, "no lady lied," so I just tossed it off as a white fib and forgot it.

"Put your hat and coat on; we will not come back to the room. The bus will leave at eight and if you miss breakfast it will be your fault." She then walked back to the dresser and laid a twenty-five-cent piece on the corner for the maid, glided to the door and was gone.

I could hurry when I had to and I didn't miss breakfast or the bus. I was on the outside seat when it pulled out of the station.

I believe that everyone on that bus had already been to the Valley before except me, and Gene reminded me to pay attention and I'd learn something. It was "Look, look," until I was sure that my neck was coming unscrewed.

That bunch of first comers stood by me all of the summer, and one of them stood up to Gene and lied so I could go on a trip.

Gene had asked, "Where in thunder is Indian Canyon?" and he had said, "Oh, it is nothing at all; I've been up there many times myself." Of course, no one had ever been up there before and Jim finally admitted to Gene that he had no idea where it was. When Bill and I hadn't shown up by midnight, the rangers were called out. But more of that later.

Mr. and Mrs. Curry sat with the driver, and took no part in the joking and laughter behind them. They had a camp to set up within the next few hours, before the sun set. They had a caretaker on the grounds, but even then, sometimes a bear would break into the kitchen and wreck the place, I had been told.

Gene was at the rear of the bus, where most of the men were, and her quick snappy answers must have pleased them. I was near the center. I certainly should've be expected to remember everything that was being told me.

"There is a huge rock up ahead and we are supposed to drive under it. The horse-drawn stage could always get through, but will the motor bus make it?"

"There is a waterfall on the left side that is different from any of the others. It splits and goes on each side of a big rock, and the spray is so thick at the height of the season that no one can get near to it; and by the time that you can get near it the snows have melted and it isn't much of a fall anymore."

I was trying to hang on to my hat. I thought it was a silly thing, when my Tam o'Shanter would have been snug and warm around my ears. Gene said that "you were supposed to be dressed properly and that being comfortable was not to be considered, otherwise people might want to travel in their bathrobes."

I also had to hang on to the side of the bus, and I guess my mouth being open most of the time, trying to answer all of the questions being asked me, was the reason I had so much mud on my tongue. Mud was in my eyes and hair and on my clothes. They were spattered. The snow had melted and left slush in the ruts, and if they were deep, the wheels threw it back along the sides, especially on the outside seats.

We were doing all of ten miles an hour and several times when we went around a curve I tried to see the side of the road and couldn't. It was like going through the air and a canyon was somewhere down there below.

They were the longest and scariest miles I had ever traveled and I hoped I would be able to come back to see some of the things they were trying to show me. It had been something like the first nickelodeon that Papa had taken me to when I was eight. Everything jumped around so much and it didn't look clear.

There was a river. You'd see it and then you didn't. There were trees without leaves and some with needles called pines. There were patches of snow and bare brown spots and rocks as big as houses on both sides of the road. One on the left was called El Capitan and it was supposed to have enough granite in it to build a road from San Francisco to New York, and there was a tall spire that no one agreed on its height.

"Do you like snow?" someone asked me.

"I don't know, I was only about four when we left New York."

I had remembered that it was white, but I had forgotten how cold it could be. The bus didn't have a top and you could see everything, and you could also get all the air from off the glaciers.

"When all the snow starts to melt up on the rim, then the falls will start to boom and roar, night and day. It will be hard to sleep at first. It will be that way until they start to dry up in the fall. Then we will have a silent Valley."

"Has anyone seen a snow plant yet? If not, it meant that there will be more snow coming."

Bridal Veil Falls, 1915. Photo by Laura White, courtesy of Yosemite National Park Archives.

I didn't look quickly enough to see where the Ribbon Falls would be and I never did get back to see it. When I left in September it was all dried up. I did get back to see Bridal Veil Falls at its best later in the season, and when we pulled into the Village I saw where the great Yosemite Falls would be when the snow began to melt.

Someone dashed into the Ranger Station, the driver disappeared into the post office, and Mr. Curry went into the hotel. We were told that we would be going in a few minutes, so no one else got off. Camp Curry was only a mile or so on up the road.

There was so much to see now that we were stopped and in the Valley proper. I just couldn't absorb it all. There was Glacier Point on the right, and North Dome on the left with the Royal Arches underneath, and Half Dome, "the Queen of the Valley," straight ahead and next to Clouds Rest, and many more points of interest. None of them seemed to be in the way of the others. It looked as though some master artist had arranged them.

During the few minutes that we waited in the bus, everybody had stopped talking. When the motor stopped, there was no reason to yell or else the spell of the Valley had started to work and everyone felt he was in the presence of something so great and wonderful that he had to be silent. No church had ever made me feel so much like singing and rejoicing, and I knew I was going to love this outdoor chapel forever and ever.[3]

When we got going again, someone asked me how I liked the trip. I said, "Terrible."

"Not half as rough as the stage would have been. Why, they have to box you in to keep you from bouncing out."

"Is Bill coming up?" another asked.

"Hope so," another answered. "He sure keeps things a-rolling with his shenanigans, always into something."

3. This could be an allusion to John Muir's writings. Muir often referred to Yosemite and wilderness in religious terms such as these.

"I'd miss that big belly-laugh of his if he didn't come," called out another.

"I'd think he would run out of shirts," said someone else. "Why, last year he had a shirt flying from every peak before the snow was off the rim."

"He's training to climb Mount Starr King. Seems like he has a deal with Pillsbury to go along with one of those movie cameras to catch him doing it."

I should have listened more carefully, and put a clamp on my tongue, but there were so many Bills. How could one more make any difference? But of course it did, and I, an unknown hiker, was actually going to challenge one of the best hikers that ever pitted his strength against the granite spires of Yosemite. But more of that later when he arrived.

The bus rounded some big trees, and everyone stopped talking again. We were there. No one said so but I could feel it. The bus slid to a stop in the slush. Mr. Curry was the first to jump out, and he threw his head back and yelled, "Welcome!"

Everyone began to move at the sound of that great voice and with all of them talking at once it was hard to catch a sentence, but I did hear Mr. Curry's voice loud and clear, "I want at least three tents up before the sun sets, two of them furnished, now get going."

Mrs. Curry was already leading the way to a building on the left, with Gene and me following. I heard her tell Gene that it would be a few days before the cook would arrive, but she was sure we could manage. One of the men would keep one of the stoves going. The caretaker cooked on a small camp stove, but it would be too small for our big crowd.

We went through the big dining room that was filled with stacked furniture and bedsteads, dressers and chairs and tables. When we had wiggled our way to the back of the room, Mrs.

Cathedral Spires, 1915. Photo by Laura White, courtesy of Yosemite National Park Archives.

Three Brothers, 1915. Photo by Laura White, courtesy of Yosemite National Park Archives.

Curry called to two of the men who had followed us and told them to clear off three of the tables and put some of the chairs around and then come to the kitchen, where she would find something else for them to do.

She was sure a wonder! In no time at all, she had Gene peeling potatoes, and me setting the tables; boxes were being opened, and the kettles were being filled with water, and a big frying pan as big as a chair seat was set on the stove. A man with a fork two feet long was stirring the potatoes that had all been sliced and dropped into the hot lard. A big handful of pepper and one of salt went into the pan and I was sure it would be ruined, but as it browned and sizzled it began to have the most tantalizing smell. In another pan as big as the first were sputtering big slices of ham.

I stacked more bread onto plates and carried them into the tables than Gene and I ever used in a week at home. And there were big jars of jam, and butter, and big pitchers of scalding hot coffee.

When they rang the gong at noon, the tables were loaded and everyone came on the run.

I had tried to keep an eye out on what was going on outside, but one window was all I could see out of as I passed from the kitchen to the tables, but every one of the men were carrying something, and the sound of hammers was everywhere. Now I wanted to run outside but I knew that I didn't dare. I was supposed to be a grown-up person, capable of holding down a job. I didn't think I fooled anyone, but I knew I was there to work and I knew that if I did my work right I'd be allowed to stay.

All that food disappeared in less than an hour, and in no time at all, I was carrying dishes back to the kitchen for Gene to wash. After I had cleared the tables and reset them, I went into the kitchen to help where I could. Mrs. Curry was glad that Gene had a watch, and I told her we had better locate our baggage and she told one of the men to go along and see that it was put in the tent that we were to occupy for the time being, the one under the oak. She told him to be sure and show us where the bath house was.

"Be back by four and we will see what we can fix that our men-folks will like," she called after us.

As we followed Jim to the stack of luggage still piled beside the bus, he said, "I sure like working for Mother Curry; she thinks of everything and wants everyone to be full and happy."

We located our trunk and suitcases, and followed him and the cart that he pushed to where a big white tent was set up.

I had noticed that a tent had been set up near the dining room, and Jim said that was the Curry tent. He showed us another one almost up. The tents were heavy and it took several men to wrestle the canvas into shape over the framework. The platforms and uprights were already in place.

"It was doubtful if they would get the third one finished," but he said the men could curl up on the floor and make believe they were camping; some of them might even curl up on the kitchen floor or the office.

He suggested that we hurry and make our bed, as the big power house was not in running order and there might not be lights for days.

He pointed out the bath house beyond the laundry and just behind the swimming pool. There wouldn't be any hot water until the laundry began to operate. There would be plenty of cold water and he said if we took any water to the tent to be sure to wrap something around the pitcher or the water would be cold in the morning.

"The only heat you will have will be the hot bricks. When ready to go to bed, you will find the oven full of them and they will help a little," he grinned. I guessed that they would a little.

He took off in the direction of the pool and when he swung the door of the wash house open and waved, we knew it was O.K. Gene acknowledged his wave and turned and stood a minute looking into the tent. There was a double bed-cot with a mattress on it, a dresser and a wash stand and some crockery and two chairs piled high with blankets, sheets, and liners.

I said I was still awfully cold and Gene said she would unpack the warm things in the morning. There wasn't time now. We'd have to make up the bed, comb our hair, and get back to the kitchen to help. "It will be warmer over there," she said and she grinned and reminded me of what Jim had said about the bricks.

"Yes, he had said they would help a little—but he didn't say how little," I answered through chattering teeth.

Gene made up the bed in a hurry, and then we went to the wash house and found it as cold as the tent had been. There was water running in the hand bowls, and Gene said probably there was a well house near or they had a small pump in the laundry and if it was well wrapped it would do until the bigger equipment was in running order.

Wells and pumps and motors were all new talk to me, so I hustled to dab some water here and there on my face, and even wiped some of the mud out of my hair. The veil that Gene had worn over her hat had protected her hair. I had asked her how old I had to be before I could wear a veil.

"Oh, a long time. You will have to wear a bridal veil first."

From the grin on her face I supposed she was kidding. I filled the pitcher and started back to the tent.

It was then that I looked up and fell in love with a rock formation across the Valley. That must be North Dome, I thought. Someone had mentioned the Arches and that would be the beautiful curving rock arches below the Dome. I was standing there so entranced that I didn't hear Gene at first.

"Come, come, you've got months to gab, and right now we have only ten minutes to get back to the kitchen."

I put the pitcher on the stand and Gene draped a big bath towel around it. Then we hurried to the kitchen, where we found Mrs. Curry and several boys busy. When I saw the big stack of potato peelings, I glanced at Gene and she had a grin a foot wide.

"We have everything about ready," Mrs. Curry greeted us. "You both can serve tonight. These boys have had good training in their homes sometime in the past, and can help me here for the time being. We just had word that some guests are coming in tomorrow, so I will want you both to start getting their tents ready in the morning. You can continue to serve the tables until I can replace. Be sure to dress warm tomorrow, for you will be out in this cold all day."

It was dark before we had finished eating and we were told that sometimes in the winter there was only about four hours of daylight and never any sun on the south side of the Valley. The talk at the table went something like this:

"Glacier Point raises straight up 3,254 feet from here, cutting off the sun, and if you want any you have to walk over to the

Arches, where it might shine for a few hours, but it isn't very warm yet."

"Well, I'll settle for a lukewarm sun rather than none at all."

"I move that the first time we get an hour in the clear and we see the sunshine over there, that we make a run for it."

Everyone at the table said, "Aye, aye," and we all had a good laugh.

When Gene and I had cleared the tables and finished the dishes, I reset the tables, Jim came up and offered to show us how to wrap the bricks, and said he would pilot us to our tent in case a bear was about.

"Quit trying to scare the girls; bears hibernate in winter."

"The females do," said someone.

"The males do, too," said another.

Well, everybody seemed to get into the discussion for about a half hour. It was the bears do this and the bears do that. I never found out who was right.

Finally, with the hot bricks wrapped in several thicknesses of newspaper, we let Jim lead the way to the tent. He said it wouldn't make much difference if the tent flaps were up or down, as long as we didn't have any food in the tent, so we didn't need to worry about the bears, and if the moon happened to shine, the view was worth a degree or two of cold. It was hard at first to think of all those rough-looking men as artists, but gradually I realized that all those who loved the Valley were artists. Their eyes became soft and misty as they would straighten up from their work and for a moment just look. Then with a sigh they would resume their lifting or heaving as though for that one moment of beauty it had been done.

Gene thanked Jim for seeing us home, and we called goodnight as he disappeared into the darkness. I knew that Gene couldn't put any chair under a door knob tonight and I was curious just what she would do, when she said out of the darkness,

"Let's get these bricks under blankets while there is some heat in them."

We felt our way around the bed and pushed them to the foot of the bed. It was so funny to be undressing in the dark. I heard Gene open a drawer and then I heard the click of the lock on the trunk and realized that she had relented at last and was feeling around in the trunk for warmer gowns. When she located me in the dark she pushed a bundle of soft, cozy warmness into my arms. Not only the new flannel gowns but the wool longies also. Funny how sub-zero weather could change a person. I thought of all the careful routine of the night before. She couldn't blame this on me. But then who would be crazy enough to stand around in the dark taking pins out of her hair with her knees knocking together?

While all these crazy thoughts were going through my head I was undressing and shoving my clothes between the blankets, even my shoes. I put the longies on and the gown over them and was in bed long before she was. I wasn't sure, but I could just know that she had folded each article of her clothes before pulling the blanket up over them. I felt a little guilty about the longies, and in feeling for the brick, I pushed my foot on her side of the bed and when I hit her I said, "I'm sorry." I turned over toward the edge again and grinned. Gene was all right sometimes. She was in bed with her longies on too.

It seemed only a minute before I realized that Gene was shaking me to get up. I don't know how long she had been up but she had the trunk open and had taken out sweaters, my wool cap, my gloves and heavy stockings, a heavy coat and a wool dress for both of us.

We left the tent laughing and warmly dressed and ready to work. It was funny the trouble I had had trying to get the longies wrapped around my ankles with one hand holding the ankle while with the other trying to pull the heavy black lisle stockings up over the wool. No matter how I tried, it was just a bunch of knobby wrinkles. My skirts were long and would hide them, but they felt awful.

"You'll only have to wear them until it warms up," Gene tried to console me. And to make matters worse, I couldn't button my shoes and had to wear my shoes with laces, and the sides didn't cover the tongue, and I was near to bawling. But worse was to come. After the cold came two weeks of snow followed by puddles with pine needles floating on top. I wasn't to know dry feet or shoes until it warmed up and I could wear tennis shoes. If there were boots for girls, I had never heard of them. At least I was warm and dry of foot that first morning and as we met the rest of the group they looked just as funny and bundled up as we did. I guess our humor was supposed to keep us warm. With all the joking, we quit talking about the cold; we just accepted it.

After breakfast, Mrs. Curry went with us to the laundry, where she showed us the shelves with linens. There were hundreds of sheets and pillow cases, also spreads; in another place there was the cleaning equipment, brooms and powders, and dustpans and the many cans and jars that are needed to keep things clean. There were large canvas baskets on wheels marked for soiled sheets, towels, etc., where we were to put the linens to be washed.

It was such a big place that the mangle was higher than my head and longer than a bed, and there were many tubs and wringers that ran by electricity and dozens of ironing boards. I was to learn a great deal about all these before summer was over, but all I wanted to do that first morning was look—I should have been listening.

Mrs. Curry had shown Gene how to load the big two-wheeled chart that she was to push around in caring for the tents. "Now, Laura," she said, "you fill your cart and meet us back of the office space where we will start. I will show Gene how I want the beds to look and she can show you."

After she had gone a few steps, she called back, "Don't load the cart too heavy, only enough for two double beds, as the carts are hard to push in slushy snow."

I was so relieved that Gene was to show me what to do for I surely didn't want to displease Mrs. Curry ever, so I just had to guess what to load up with.

By the time I got there, the one tent had been finished, and Mrs. Curry had left. She was like that all summer, here and there, keeping everything on the move, smiling and saying a few kind words to everyone.

Gene gave me my first lesson in the second tent. I had never had to make a bed in my life. I didn't know there was so much to it. First, I was shown the two sizes of hems: the big one always went to the top, smooth side up, it was tucked in all around so that when it was folded back over the blanket, the next sheet was smooth side down; the center crease had to be in the center of the bed so that there was sufficient sheet hanging on both sides of the bed to tuck under; the bottom sheet was tucked in all around (tight as a drum), the top sheet only at the bottom until the blankets were on and then a little of both blankets and sheet were tucked in near the foot. That fold had to be on an angle so it wouldn't pull loose and no wrinkles anywhere. Then the spread was put on, to hang even all around. Last but not least in importance came the two pillows. First the pillow had to be shaken to equalize the feathers, then laid flat on the bed and pounded with your two arms (from the elbows to the fists) until it was hard enough to stand alone, against the head of the bed. In my little notebook in the summer I had written, "made up sixty double beds to-day." That would have been 120 pounded pillows. To me that was the hardest part of the job. That first day, of course, we only made up about ten tents before it began to get dark. We left candles in a drawer with matches for those who might come before the lights were in operation.

The beds made and the floor swept; the dresser and wash stand dusted and with clean scarfs, every day; the hand bowl scrubbed and dried; no water in the pitchers until the weather had warmed, unless the tent was to be occupied and the pitcher wrapped; fresh soap in the soap dish (a kind the chipmunks didn't like); two bath towels and two hand towels and two wash cloths; the commode emptied and cleaned and the lid in place; the flaps of the tent folded back neatly and tied, and a quick look around that all was as it should be. Then that meant that the tent was finished. Then you rolled your cart to the next tent and did the whole thing all over again.

Rest rooms were located every so far about the camp, and really people preferred to use them, so it wasn't so bad. When the hot weather came, I soon found out that all people don't smell alike. No wonder animals run from us. During the rush season, purely for self-preservation, I used to step inside the tent, grab a handful of covers, and flip them over the foot of the bed, and duck outside again. By the time I had gathered up the change of sheets and other linen, the air had cleared. That few seconds made a lot of difference. It was a good idea, except for once. I presumed, of course, that the guests had gone to breakfast or on a hike and that the bed was empty. I grabbed the covers and had them halfway to the bottom of the bed when I discovered that the bed was not empty. They screamed and I fled. People shouldn't be so skinny.

There were 500 more tents put up that first two months and Gene and I made them livable. By then the other girls had arrived and we were given sections of our own. If many of our tents were empty for the day or the guests had gone on a hike or a mule trip and we finished early, we either helped the others get through or we would go to the laundry to help for an hour or two. Many a dear helped me get through early because they knew how I loved to hike and would take the trail if only for an hour or two. Often, we would all help each other and then go to the kitchen and pick up some food and take off for a moonlight hike or a picnic.

There was no time for picnics or hikes the first month or two. There was a big job to be done and we all pitched in and saw that it was done. There were all those new tents to be put up. Trees had to be cut down and big rocks had to be dynamited before the ground could be leveled to put up the tent frame and flooring. I believe that every man had a hammer and there was a big racket all day. The dining room was enlarged, and a porch was added on three sides; small limbs with the bark left on were used for upright rafters and fragrant pine limbs with the needles left on were spread over the top for shade and replaced often so that the diners always had the fresh smell of cedar or pine to enjoy while eating. Also in the summer tons of pine needles were raked over the grounds to keep the dust down, and especially around the office area. It was like walking on a cushion. In this same circle was the famous fire that burned almost continuously. New logs were stacked "tepee like" each afternoon and in the evening it was lighted and it would burn all night and a great part of the next day. A hundred or more reclining camp chairs circled the fire and were all in use, except at meal times or the wee hours before dawn. To lie back in one of them on a moonlit night and listen to the Yosemite Falls roaring, and the crackle of the pitch in the logs, and watch the shadows on the cliffs as the moon moved over and out of the Valley, was a memory that millions have taken away with them.

Another big memory people took away with them was the Fire Fall that started as soon as the weather had quieted down and men could be sent up the Ledge Trail in safety to gather up a large quantity of pine cones and loose bark. In the early evening, it would be set afire and allowed to burn down to coals. In time for the nine o'clock call from the Stentor, "Let her fall." Then the embers would be pushed slowly over the brink to fall a thousand feet onto the ledge below. All lights in the camp would be out and that falling fire that lasted for several minutes was always a thrilling sight. Many of us would go across into the meadow to watch the fall. Music has been written about it, also poems and songs. It was always inspiring.

It was about a week after we had settled into our temporary quarters, and Gene and I were crossing an entrance road by the side of our tent, when a horse and rider dashed into the road and nearly into us. The rider was a tall, dark-haired man, and he reined in the horse so hard it reared up on its hind legs and snorted. We all had a bad scare.

Danger either threw Gene into cool-headed control and sensible action, or angry, senseless hysteria. This time she screamed at him a hundred things she thought he was. He had dismounted and had the horse under control and kept agreeing with her. "Yes, ma'am, that's what I am and I am sorry. I didn't know there were any women in the camp," et cetera, et cetera. Gene's hat had fallen off and the light was on her hair.

"Madam, have you ever been in Montana? I've seen that head of hair somewhere before, and once seen, it could never be forgotten."

"Yes," said Gene, and of course the flattery had its effect. "And pray tell me where you have seen this head, now that you didn't succeed in knocking it off my shoulders."

He laughed a great-throated laugh and said, "You were a bride, or should I say, a young mother." He glanced over at me and said, "This must be the young lady that was the noisy one, screaming all the time." Then he laughed again.

"I brought a deer to your cabin," and he was looking back at

Gene again. "As a friendly gesture and you screamed, 'Take it away, take it away!' I believe you were scared of the first Indian you had ever seen, and me in a breech-clout, and as for me, I had only ever seen a few white women. Our women had to be quiet and keep their babies quiet for the safety of the tribe. I didn't like white women and their screaming kids and I still don't." He looked my way and grinned. I grinned back and knew we were going to be friends. He was the only man who had ever talked to Gene like that and was getting away with it.

He turned back to Gene again. "I finally convinced you that I meant you no harm, and that your husband, who I had met on the trail, had told me to bring the deer to the cabin. I also told you that if at any time you needed help, to hang a white cloth on the tree limb in front of your door. On Christmas day, you did just that. Do you remember now?"

Gene's face lit up with remembering and she went toward him and offered her hand, and she was all smiles. He took it and said, "I must go now, will see you later," and smiling he tipped his hat and led his horse through the camp to the office building.

I was all curious, and when we were inside the tent, I asked what he meant. Gene sat down on the bed and because of her dreamy look I curled up on the trunk for I could see that she had a story building up, which wasn't often.

After a big sigh, she said slowly, "It was your second Christmas. You were thirteen months old, and I had been homesick and blue. Back on the plantation, we would work for weeks cooking and baking and decorating, and we would have a big tree that would reach to the ceiling, all atwinkle and bright, and stacks of presents, and there would be dozens of youngsters, cousins and kin from miles around, whooping it up all over the place, and everyone happy, and there I was in a cabin on an Indian reservation with bars on the one window to keep out the mountain lions. Your Papa had dropped a piece of surveying equipment on the trail the night before and had gone to look for it. He had said that if he didn't find it, he would have to send all the way to Chicago or Washington, D.C., for another, no tree, no presents, just loneliness.

"I looked out of the window and saw your Papa staggering through the snow, with his two hands over his face. I ran out to him, and his face was all bloody, and his groans were terrible. A limb had snapped back into his face, knocking his eye out, and he was holding it in his hands.

"I was frantic and helpless and I remembered what the Indian boy had said, so I grabbed a pillow case and hung it on the limb as he had said to do.

"It seemed but a few minutes when I saw him racing his horse over the snow. He took charge immediately and seemed to know what to do. He forced the eye back into the socket and said there would be trouble unless it was properly cared for right away. I was told to hurry and pack, for the one train would be going through about dark. The hospital was in Kalispell, where he had taken some training a few years back.[4]

"He yelled at me to pack, pack everything.

"He dashed outside and came back with a piece of bark that he put in your Papa's mouth, and soon the groans stopped.

"He grabbed the axe and was gone again and from the window I saw him dragging two limbs that he had stripped of their side sprigs. Then he tied the limbs to the horse, one on each side. He came in and dragged the trunk outside and put it on the limbs and tied it. I was going to leave the wet wash, but he grabbed it up and rolled it in a sheet and said I could do it at the hospital.

"He gathered up some kindling and paper and a handful of matches, saying that 'white man's fire was quicker,' and put the

4. Kalispell emerged as a railroad town at the turn of the twentieth century. Today, the city serves as a gateway to Glacier National Park.

bundle on top of the trunk, and leading the horse to your Papa, called for me to follow. Seeing them going away brought me up with a start, and I gathered you up in some blankets and followed.

"By the time I had caught up with them, they had reached the tracks a mile or two from the cabin. Parsons had a fire going. The night had come down quick and way off in the prairie I could see the headlights of the train.

"I left your Papa in the hospital in Kalispell and after seeing that the washing was done and he was resting as well as could be expected, I repacked the trunk proper and dressed both of us for traveling respectable, and we went on to California to stay with his aunt, until he would be able to follow.

"I visited with Auntie many times after that. She was the one that I came to Yosemite with when you were three years old." Gene shook herself as though coming out of a trance and said, "Just imagine finding someone up here, out of the past, like that.

"Just what did we come down to the tent for?" she asked.

"We were going to do the laundry and do some ironing," I reminded her.

"Oh, yes, but let us move instead. The tents are up in the Jungle Town. I was told that the girls will have the row facing the road. Let us go and pick one out before supper."

So we went down the trail and picked out one with a perfect view of South Dome and the Arches. I sometimes get my way.

I unmade one bed and made up the other while Gene lugged the clothes in her arms, which lightened the trunk so we could drag it down the path ourselves. We liked the location because it was farther from the center of camp. The gong rang out and we hurried to supper and forgot to say anything about us moving.

I guess it was because on my way a couple of the boys grabbed us and pushed us under a snow laden limb. They shook the tree and the snow fell on us nearly covering us. They would leave us to scramble out the best way we could. It happened many times those first weeks in May, and being in fun, we screamed to please them, and then laughed with them. We had to shake like a dog coming out of water. Then they would holler and say, "Look at the girls! They're doing the hoochie-coochie!"

At supper Mr. Curry announced that every man was to get a broom or a shovel and get the snow off the tent roofs, that all unoccupied tent flaps were to be tied, and that he was sure the quiet snow fall was over and that a freeze or a blow could easily make a lot of extra work for all.

Gene and I went back to our new location, and finished putting the things in the bureau drawers, and then we went to bed.

About midnight, we heard a terrible crash, and then a lot of hollowing. We slipped our coats over our gowns and stepped into our shoes and went to see what was up. We saw a lot of lanterns up near where our former tent house was and went up there. We found that the big oak limb had crashed down through the tent onto the bed and the people naturally supposed we were underneath. One of the boys had crawled in under the canvas to see if we were still alive. What a cheer went up when they saw us coming on the path. They danced around us and all wanted to touch us to make sure we were really us.

Before I fell asleep I said, "Gene, what made you move today?"

"Oh, just a hunch," and then real cross, "go to sleep."

She had saved our lives like this once before by moving us out of danger, but she had been real cross when I had asked her about it again. But I kept still and tried to think of the strange side that she had to her.

It had started to snow the first day of May and it snowed until the fifteenth. At first, we had all welcomed the snow because it meant a drop in temperature. At first, everyone was throwing snowballs but after the first hundred it became tiresome. But the beauty of that first snow we all enjoyed. It came down as light as goose feathers, and soon every stick, tree, and board had several inches of new snow on it. The whole Valley was turned into a fairyland of white.

One afternoon the grapevine let us know that we were missing something behind the auditorium, so we sneaked over to see. I have never seen anything like that snowman. It was five or six feet high and about three to four feet thick. It was sitting on a log with both legs bent at the knees. The face was a work of art. Deep-set eyes and bushy eyebrows and a pipe in its mouth. Both hands were clasped over the stomach and each finger was perfectly made.

"Hey, where's all my help?" Mr. Curry bellowed.

When he saw the snowman, he looked around and said, "What, no cameras?"

There was a mad rush for the cameras. Gene and I ran to get our carts and there was a good picture made of us. The snowman was pictured on all sides and with every one of us and then ten boys showed up in bathing suits including Bill Pontynen, a young man I had not met before but would be friends with for the rest of my life.

At supper that night, Jim said, "Camp is really started now that Bill is here. When I saw the bathing suits, I said to myself it looks like one of his ideas, so I looked around and sure enough he was standing right there by Laura. If there are shoes and pants on the donkey after supper, you can be sure he is all steamed up for the summer."

I was so surprised that someone new had come into camp and I hadn't noticed him that I just sat and stared.

"He is not too tall, but all muscle and strength; and he can climb; he is too busy for girls, hikes only with boys." Then they all looked at me and I could feel my face burning.

Well, the rest of the meal was a review of all the stunts he had done in the past, and someone said that when he and his friend Will came up their first year, they were called "Jiblets" and "Joblets," but now that they were in the first year of college, maybe they wouldn't let us call them that.

Well, I was miffed. I think that was the word for it. I was not a bit boy-crazy and if he didn't want to speak to me, it was all right with me. I wouldn't speak to him. So there.

"Your nose is out of joint," Gene said later, "the only girl in camp and he didn't even see you."

To be the first on a peak and climb a mountain before breakfast while the rest of us shivered and shook to keep warm looked silly to me. Then, of course, I had never seen a hero nor had I set any records, so what would I know about the pride of accomplishment?

Nor did I feel any better the next morning, rushing over to breakfast, to see a group of boys crowding around someone and I went to look. There was this here fellow and two others. They had their eyes blackened round with soot to prevent the sun-glare off the snow, I was told later. They had on khaki and high boots and carried hiking sticks and gear. They were answering questions, "Yes, the Ledge had been conquered. They had climbed up at sunup and slid back down in time for breakfast," and, "Oh, yes," he had "left a shirt on Sentinel Dome."

Envy, kid stuff, whatever it was, I heard myself say, "Think you are the only one who can hike?" And the minute I said it I could have bitten my tongue off. Hadn't I said the night before that I wouldn't speak to him, and here I was, I had actually challenged him.

He looked at me as though I were a flea to be squashed. His big brown eyes glared behind the soot ring. His words were short and sharp.

"Can you?"

"I can go anywhere you can go," I snapped back.

He stared at me for the first time as though he had just realized I was a girl. "Why, I could break your fool neck the first trip out." And he started to his tent.

I wasn't going to let him curse me so I yelled out, "When do we start?"

The war was on.

"She can do it if she says so," said Parsons.

"She's soft, and green, and a girl and I bet she is yellow," answered one of Bill's friends.

We all started for the dining room and it didn't help when Hal walked up beside me and leaned over and snickered, "You had better get in some practice."

I gave him a dirty look, but he only laughed.

George came up and took my arm and said, "You know we will have to do something to fellows who pick on someone half their size, and a girl at that. I don't think his mother raised him right."

Everyone got to laughing again, but something had happened to me. I decided right there, I'd go anywhere that show-off went, and if I broke my neck—well, it was my neck.

The kidding got worse, and I know that Bill was trying to evade me every chance he could. Well, I wasn't chasing him, and that was easy. He had charge of the running of the washing machines and dryers in the laundry and I made it a point never to look in that direction when I had to get linens. However, every time we met by accident and others were around they would speak up and ask him when he was going out to break my neck.

"When I get all my shirts up where they belong, I'll take care of her. Will and I have lots of places to go first," he would answer them. He never looked at me and I never cared.

It was all of a month before he was forced into setting a trip. A lady had challenged him, and "he couldn't refuse," someone told him.

So one Sunday afternoon he started up the road about five feet in front of me and I was as mad at him as I was at the bunch of so-called friends who had forced this hike on me. The fact that I had brought all this on myself didn't make it any easier to accept. We were headed toward Mirror Lake.

"There's no hike up there," someone yelled.

"Maybe he is going to drown her in the lake," someone else joined in.

We answered not a word.

As for me, I had said too much already. I had blown off my big mouth and I wanted to put my foot in it, and I was sure everybody else knew I was a big phony.

As for Bill, he was the best hiker Yosemite had ever had. I could imagine him telling his pal Will, "Just wait until I get through with this smart aleck, she'll wish she had never seen a trail."

I wasn't so dumb I couldn't learn. I watched him as he walked steady and breathed deep, his body swinging in a rhythm that I couldn't achieve because I had to wear a corset with whalebone stakes every half inch from armpits to thighs. But even then, I pledged myself to go wherever he went.

We passed Mirror Lake and I don't think he or I even looked at it. I followed him on up the Tenaya Zig Zags to the top.

He stood and looked about him for a few minutes, took a deep breath, and talked as though he had to, "Not bad for a beginner." Looking at his watch, he continued, "Just about time to make it back in time for supper. I think I will run back."

"That wasn't in the bargain, so run if you want to. I know my way back," and I tried to sound as unpleasant as he did.

I let him get out of sight, and then I took off at about the same speed. It got real dark before we reached camp so I had been able to quicken my pace and I had shortened the space between us so that I was close enough behind him to hear someone in the

bunch of boys waiting at the entrance call out, "Here comes Bill,
but where is Laura?"

"She decided to walk back," Bill answered.

They were sure surprised when I called out, "Here I am!"

"How come he ran and you walked and got here the same
time?"

"Oh, I am lighter and get over the ground faster," and I went
on to the washroom to get ready for supper.

I had a feeling that as far as this hike went I had won. What
might happen in the future could be different.

It was sometime into May when someone reported that they had
found a snow plant close to Happy Isles Trail. Of course, everybody wanted to see it. Some flowers have a little red in them,
others are all red with green leaves, but no flower gives you quite
the surprise that the snow plant does. There is no green, it is a
fiery red, and at first you think it looks as if it were made of wax,
and then you think it resembles an asparagus, then you look
closer and see the little clusters along the stalk, something like
hyacinth. I guess there is no describing it, it usually has the snow
as a background and that makes the red look redder.

Usually someone piles sticks or stones around it to keep people from stepping on it. Being a national park, it is on the protected list and there is a fifty-dollar fine for picking it. Anyway,
it gives you pleasure to see and what more can any flower do for
you?

No matter what was happening, once the work was done and
we gathered around the fireplace or weather permitting the outside fire, the Valley was the chief topic of conversation.

The merits of one piece of granite against another, as to its
art, its height, its history, was it climbable, what were its dif-
ficulties? Each piece of granite had its own history, each had its
own type of line and beauty. To different people it meant differ-

Nevada Falls Bridge, 1915. Photo by Laura White, courtesy of Yosemite National Park Archives.

ent things. The same things could be said about the falls, some preferred the gracefulness of Vernal, others the rampaging roaring wildness of Nevada, others the mightiness of Yosemite, and others the mistiness of Bridal Veil Falls.

The Domes were always a big topic, and Half Dome in particular. If you were new in the Valley, you had to be told how George Anderson[5] always went barefooted and climbed like a monkey and how he helped his father, who drilled the first holes for the eyebolts on the north side, and how Anderson finished putting in the last ones into which he tied ropes way back in. Hikers were then able to get to the top. The winter storms soon rotted the ropes and tore them loose and it had not been climbed since. Probably never would be for it was an angle and over 600 feet of bare granite from the overhanging rock to the floor of the Valley.

5. George Anderson was the first person on record to summit Half Dome in 1875.

All of these mountain folks with the light of the Scottish Highlands in their eyes knew and loved John Muir, who had died the year before. All of the older ones had something nice to say about him and said that California had been the real loser.[6]

"Yes, he died of a broken heart," said an old timer.

"A man dying of a broken heart?" spoke up one of the younger men. "I thought that was only for young ladies."

The older man's face flushed with anger. "Well, John Muir could have, for he loved this Valley as few people have, and he spent most of his life fighting to get this beautiful place set aside so that other people could come here and enjoy it. He called the sheep the 'hoofed locust' because they devoured the flowers. If they had had the protective law for flowers then as now, those sheep breakfasts would have cost millions of dollars. The sheep ate all growth right down to the ground."

Muir traveled and lectured and wrote articles and got the people to thinking that there were other generations coming that would like to enjoy the mountains. He traveled the backcountry alone with a chunk of bread and a tin cup tied to his belt, and a handful of tea leaves in a pocket. He slept where the setting sun found him.

He loved the Hetch Hetchy Valley almost as much as here and he tried to save it for the people, too, and when they voted to dam the canyon and flood the meadows, it broke his heart. The beauties he had enjoyed would never be seen by anyone else again.

Future generations would never know the grand coloration of the lowlands; it would be covered by a lake.

6. Popular legend has it that John Muir died shortly after plans to dam the Hetch Hetchy Valley in northern Yosemite were approved. The controversial reservoir project still provides water to the city of San Francisco.

The old timer got up and moved away in silence and we all knew we had heard a sermon from his heart.

The seasons of Yosemite had their admirers, too. There were those who preferred the cold of the winters and a white world. Others liked the wild colors of the fall, but most of them settled for the beauty of spring, when the falls were at their best. The azaleas along the river, the lunar rainbows[7] when the moon was right, and on and on it would go, and I never tired of listening.

Many of the first comers made an effort to beautify our tents, they brought carved bark baskets with ferns planted in them to hang on the outside beams, and there were two large log seats to put beside the door, and odd shaped pieces of bark or rock until certainly we had a beautiful and interesting tent garden. If we weren't happy, we sure should have been.

The laundry people had arrived and soon after May 1st the big tubs were tumbling and the dryers were wringing out clothes. Then the loads were dumped into big canvas carts and pushed over to the shaking tables where a group of people were always shaking the linens and making them pop, and laughing and talking, and didn't mind getting tired.

I learned to take a damp roll of cloth and loosen it a little and run my finger and thumb along the small hem of the nap, then take the two corners and shake it and it would pop, then lay it across a rod. After there were about a hundred piled up, I'd carry the pile over to the mangle, on the feeder side. When all the napkins to be ironed that day were on the pole in front of my chair, I would sit down and start feeding them into the rollers. I would

7. The lunar rainbow, also known as a "luna-bow" (as mentioned later in the narrative) or "moonbow," occurs when moonlight is strong enough to create a rainbow in the mist created by waterfalls. Yosemite's many falls paired with the arid summer climate make luna-bows more common than in other areas.

spread the napkin on the first roller, and it would roll out of sight onto unseen rollers and come out at the other side, hot as blazes. Gene would pick it off, fold it and stack it before the next one was showing. If I had fed faster than she would fold, the napkins would fall off the rollers and get wrinkled. After we learned the proper timing, we never dropped any.

Mrs. Curry was very firm in telling us to watch for the napkins from other places around the world, and to see that they did not get stacked in with her napkins for her tables. It was surprising how many people had helped themselves to table napkins: pick them up in one place and leave them in another. We would stack the snitched napkins in a separate pile and any of the help could take them and have a memento of Mexico or Europe. Usually they were lovely linen and the heat would bring out such beautiful designs.

The sheets were the hardest and the hottest. Gene and I worked out a rhythm the rest of them never equaled. Of course, two fast feeders had to feed the damp sheets in at the other side. We would pick the hot sheet off of the roller and hold it tightly until the other end came through, then flip it if necessary so that the two raw edges were on the inside, then pick up the lower fold and put it even with the top fold and give a good yank, one of us would step forward and give our corner to the other, and quickly snatch the fold, then the other would step forward and give her handful of corners to the other who then turned and laid the perfectly ironed sheet on the stack behind her. Of course, all double sheets were done at the same time and the single sheets were done at separate times. All sheets in the occupied tents were changed every day, so on a day at the height of the season it could well mean 2,000 sheets and that meant that the laundry was a place for strong arms and a quick eye. We never dropped a sheet or had a wrinkled sheet. If during this system our fingers ever met, it would almost knock us off our feet, the shock was terrific. They said it was only static electricity and would not do any real damage.

I was often asked to work on the towel table, where the piles of ironed face towels were evened up and racked up on the shelves. I really preferred the laundry to the tents but there were no tips and no afternoons off so I never asked for a transfer.

Gene and I had been warned to stay away from a certain area that was being prepared for new tents because of dynamiting and flying rocks. One day Gene called to me to get her some more sheets (because I was the youngest I was not supposed to get tired and my legs were supposed to be glad for the exercise). I often ran to the laundry and carried back an armload instead of using the cart. We were working behind this danger area, but not seeing any men, I supposed they were through for the day and I cut across to save time.

I had gone a few hundred feet when Parsons jumped from behind a huge boulder, grabbed me and jerked me behind the rock and threw himself on top of me. Just then the blast went off and dirt and rocks showered down all around us.

When it was over, I found myself the center of an angry mob: "Beat her!" "Spank her!" "Give her a wallop for me, crazy dern kid!" etc. I was shaken and lambasted, and I wouldn't have blamed them if they had spanked me, but I was too scared to care what they did to me. Later, my one-time friends brought me candy and said they were sorry they had yelled at me so, but they had expected me to be killed right in front of their eyes. If Parsons had not acted as quickly as he did, I guess I would have been.

I had good reason to be grateful to Parsons more than once. Early in May he had come down the road after dark and found me standing in the snow in my bare feet. I was crying my heart out. Wet feet all day and hot bricks at night had brought on a bad case of chilblains. Someone had said to stand in the snow barefooted and I was doing just that. He grabbed me up and deposited me on the bed in the tent. He grabbed a towel and patted my feet dry and wrapped a blanket around my knees and feet and told me to sit right there as he was going to the Village to get me something for the feet.

It was the only time I heard swearing that summer, but I was bawling and didn't sound good either.

He was gone less than an hour. He said he was sorry to be so long but he had to get the druggist out of bed and wait for him to dress. He had a bottle of black liquid, and he patted it on my swollen feet, all the time telling me about the herbs that made up the stuff in the bottle. He told me to put some on night and morning. Then he bandaged my feet with pieces of sheet he had brought along, and then he kept telling me stories about his boyhood in Montana and on the Flathead Reservation, and said he was fortunate that he had been born after the mothers had stopped tying boards to their babies' heads, or everybody would be able to tell in a minute that he was a fierce flathead savage. Of course, he got me to laughing. He had also brought along a pair of his shoes for me to wear over the bandages until the swelling had gone down. I wore his shoes over a week, and I sure kept my feet off the hot bricks.

The falls, especially Yosemite, kept getting louder and louder, prettier and prettier. We would see it each morning, after listening to its thunder all night. We talked falls most of the time. Finally, with most of the work caught up, a big group got off on a Sunday, and it was decided that we would make a try for the top of Yosemite Falls.

The falls were at their best, and the sun was bright, so that those who had cameras took them and George took his ukulele strung on a cord around his neck.

At the start of the trail everyone was staggering along, laughing all the time. There were no records to make. It was a trip for fun, and everyone did their part to add to it. They would get in each other's way, begging for a lift and declaring that if they took one more step they would drop dead, but nobody paid any attention. For most of them it was their first trial of climbing steadily and their leg muscles rebelled. Since everybody felt the same they just kept trudging along, lifting one foot and setting it down, then doing the same with the other. A few of them did give out and go back, but six of us persisted to the top.

When we got to the place in the trail where the mist was so heavy we knew we would get drenched, we stopped only for a minute. George sang out as he slipped his ukulele under his shirt.

"There is no denying
If you be mountain born
You hear the high hills calling."

He grabbed Rose's hand and they made a run for it. Frank grabbed Gene's hand and she screamed as they disappeared into the spray. The wind was blowing part of that 1,430 feet of falls right at us. Hal grabbed my hand and we dashed after the others.

There was still some climbing to do, the only difference was that being wet and cold there was less joking. Everyone was eager to get to the top, and get a fire going. We got there and started looking for fallen timber and dead limbs, and soon had a roaring fire going. We danced around the fire singing and eating from our lunch boxes. Oh, those wonderful lunches, big, thick slices of bread with thick slices of fried ham in them and pickles and olives and boiled eggs and fruit. Seven thousand feet up in the air is a wonderful place to eat such a lunch.

After watching the fire die down, someone suggested that we had better start back, the sun was hurrying over El Capitan and we had to decide how we would go back. George and Hal were for going across the Yosemite Creek and east to North Dome and back by the Tenaya Zig Zags, but Frank and Gene were for taking the shorter route, getting wet again and being back in camp before dark. The thought of bucking seven-foot drifts was too much for them.

The minute they had mentioned North Dome, I was for going with George and Hal, and Rose said "O.K." too.

"See that Laura gets back," Gene called as we started out.

"She'll be there," Hal yelled back at her.

The creek was a roaring torrent as it rushed to jump out into the space and form the big fall. At one time, it had been a straight drop into the Valley, but the centuries had eaten away the wall until now it was three falls, and no doubt will change again as the years roll along. The upper fall jumps 1,430 feet, the middle 675 and the lower 320; one of the world's highest.

When we hit the drifts, our pace slackened until it stopped altogether. Hal and George both said they were beginning to hate women, and they got the big idea that if they ran away and left us that we would make a bigger effort to keep up. They went clear out of sight, but Rose and I had been pulled out of so many snow holes that we didn't think we could go on.

Rose threw her arms up and flopped into the snow and said, "Now I can freeze to death in peace."

I took one look at her peaceful face and flopped down beside her.

Sometime later I was jerked to my feet, out of my frozen dreaming, shoved and bullied into motion. "I promised Gene I would get you home—so help me—as a hiking pal you are the bunk. I hope Bill takes you out and breaks your neck—you find someone else to be responsible for you."

A little later on he said, "You belly-ached so much to be on top of North Dome, well here we are. Now that you have seen it, it's as big a fraud as you are. Here, Rose, get a picture of this namby-pamby on her precious Dome." There had been no climb, the back was level with the top or nearly so.

It could have been a stick, a gun, or just his pointer finger. I don't know, but he said march and I did.

After a few miles, I was tired of being pushed home and said so, when wham—up I went and found myself across his shoulder like a sack of potatoes, head down. We made splendid time and I stood it as long as I could. I felt I was passing out, and yelled quits, and he let me down and went back to the pushing method.

When we got to the Tenaya Zig Zags, something wonderful happened, I got my second wind and took off on my own. I reached camp long before them and was completely trail-broken and determined to learn to hike or bust.

Later at the campfire, Hal came up and said he was sorry he had been so rough.

I said, "Forget it, I had it coming to me."

"You really mean that?"

"Sure, why not?"

"Let's go over and do some bowling to prove it and you can get even that way."

Later, while getting ready for bed, Gene said, "Better watch your language, I had to explain to one of the guests that you were not using profanity, that the boy's name was Hal."

It dawned on me, that every time that Hal knocked the clubs down, I would jump and yell, "Oh, Hal!"

When I went to tie back the tent flaps after putting out the lights, I thought as I looked up at North Dome, you are pretty but for a climb you're a washout. Little did I know that it would be that Dome that would nearly claim a life before the season was over. "Don't tell anybody, unless I don't come back," Bill had said.

Speaking of Bill, I hadn't seen him except at a distance since our first hike up the Zig Zags. I rather think the boys had teased him a lot because of running off and leaving me as he did. Besides, he was probably still finding peaks to hang his shirts on.

Then one evening he came to where I was sitting by the fire and asked very nicely if I'd like to take a try at the Ledge. There was no rooting section either to egg us on or to cheer.

"The melting snows make a problem at times," he said, "but the handholds are handy and the footing solid." The ledge was on the forbidden lists, but we made it to the top the next day which was Sunday. Once on top, Bill said that if we ran along the rim to the top of the four-mile trail west we could get back in time for supper.

I still felt that he would have liked to find a climb that I would have backed down on, but the bitterness was gone. He probably remembered that he had acted pretty mean and he really wasn't a devil. Well, I wasn't so proud of my unladylike talk either, so the apologies were made silently and accepted the same way.

He walked so fast that sometimes his back disappeared, and I am sure that he must have stopped to let me catch up, although he never said so.

I caught up with an old man coming down grade with the help of a cane. I stopped to say hello. He smiled and said, "I wish I could come down as easy as you kids do."

"Just loosen up and strike out like this," I said. I took a big step, landed on a smooth stone, and fell right on my face. When I picked myself up, he was looking at me with a twinkle in his eyes.

"I guess I'll keep on going the way I am, Miss."

Was I glad that Bill was way ahead and hadn't seen my mishap.

I caught up with Bill at Bridal Veil Falls and we started on a dog trot to the main road of the Valley. The roads were deep in dirt and the drop from 7,000 feet to 4,000 feet had made me feel sticky and dirty. We reached the main road and I heard a loud buzzing.

Bill stopped and turned around and said, "Gosh, I forgot about those devils, we will have to make a run for it. Keep your mouth shut and good luck."

By that time that black cloud of hungry female mosquitoes had surrounded us. They wanted to lay a lot of eggs and they wanted our blood. The only thing we could try to do was to try to keep them out of our mouths.

I had opened my mouth to answer Bill but the mosquitoes were too fast for me and I nearly choked. I began to flail my arms and really run, but the burning bites mixing with my sweat got in my eyes and I thought, "What a way to die!" I could make out Bill ahead of me and his arms were going like a windmill and his bare back was black. I heard another noise behind me and thought it another swarm.

I felt myself being lifted up and up until I was sitting on a woman's lap and she was wiping my face with her handkerchief. I saw Bill turn and swing up on the running board of the bus. The driver sped up the bus and outran the black swarm of 'skeeters. By slowing down to pick us up, many of the passengers were bitten but their only concern seemed to be for us. I never had a chance to thank the man who had lifted me up into the bus, but if he reads this, I want him to know that he was as brave as Casey Jones any day, and please accept my thanks.

The sight of blood has been known to stop many a feud, and I am sure that was the case with us. Seeing us come into camp so bloody really did worry some of them and although some of the kidding did continue it wasn't full of bitterness.

We hiked alone and with others. We seemed to be coming or going every free minute. I would often slip away alone and up the Ledge Trail when I had only an hour to sit on a projection of rock and watch the Valley below and just look and love it all. I

Laura, Bill, and friend on Castle Rock, 1915. Courtesy of Yosemite National Park Archives.

took a picture of a rock that resembled a castle, and used to say to myself, "I'm going up to my castle." I was so tired of moving around and I knew that this too would come to an end and we would be going somewhere else. I used to dream that no matter where I went, I could always close my eyes and say to myself, "I have a castle on a ledge with the most beautiful view in the world."

Groups were going to Happy Isles for picnics just as soon as the weather was comfortable. These picnics were on Sunday and included most of the laundry crew. The boys would take charge and give us watermelons until we couldn't swallow another piece, or a corn feed and they would say you have to eat until both ears got butter on them. The only trouble was that the wasps would settle on the greasy corn till you imagined they were sliding down your throat with the butter. The girls would get steaks and potatoes and onions and tomatoes from the kitchen and have a steak fry.

Afterward, we would sit around and sing for an hour or two, some of them had fine voices, some couldn't carry a note, but we all sang the old favorites, like "Suwannee River," "Old Black Joe," "Sweet and Low," "Yankee Doodle," "Tenting to Night," and many others. Someone started to sing the parody of "I need sympathy, I need sympathy, for the mosquitoes bite me, from my ankles up to my knees, we were ready to get out and give the Isles back to them." If the moon was in the right place for a luna-bow, we would follow the trail up to Vernal Falls, the spray and wind coming down the side canyon blew the mosquitoes away.

Bill was often part of the group and he suggested once that we all go down to the garbage pits to watch the bears eating. Of course, we'd better wait until the ground dried out good because we would have to lie down on our stomachs to watch them, so everybody agreed to let him set a date.

Speaking of food reminds me of the wonderful meals we had at Camp Curry. The cooks had arrived. I especially remember the grand breakfasts and how Gene and I ran as fast as the rest when the gong rang.

After a cold night and a cold wash-up in the mornings, the first we would notice as we neared the kitchen was the smell of delicious bacon and ham and the rich aroma of hot bubbling coffee and the crispy sweet smell of hot cakes. We would go to our table and strip off our heavy coats, mitts, and knit caps and put them on the back of the chairs, and with everyone talking at once it was just like one big family.

What a loaded table greeted us. There were eight at a table, and hardly an inch that wasn't loaded with food. At one corner was a big platter of eight eggs and big slices of crisp bacon, at the opposite corner was a platter of eggs and slices of juicy ham. The other two corners had platters of golden crispy hot cakes, then there was a platter of breakfast steaks and two platters of golden-brown toast and at each plate a bowl of oatmeal steaming hot for a starter. Of course, there was a big pitcher of steaming hot coffee and one of milk and there were jams or jelly or butter and in season fruits or melons.

I never remember any of that food going back to the kitchen. The meal hour was soon over for us and who couldn't work hard with such good food under his belt. The guests often lingered over their meals late in the morning unless they wanted to go for a hike and for them were the famous box lunches of which hundreds were made up each morning on order. There were always two or three sandwiches, a couple boiled eggs, fruit, delicious pickles and olives and a chunk of cheese.

The tables for dinner were equally loaded, there would be stews, large serving dishes with two kinds of vegetables besides potatoes, pies, soup, salads, and dessert. How those cooks must have loved to cook.

The suppers were also substantial, usually huge steaks, roasts, fried chicken, French-fried potatoes or mashed, two kinds of natural vegetables, not mixed as they often were for dinner. They even served puddings and ice cream. There was certainly no reason for anyone to say they were hungry in Camp Curry.

There might have been a little fault-finding by people who had the habit but never over the food. One would think that people would put on weight with such quantities of food. They might if they sat around, but who could sit around in Yosemite. I actually lost weight, but then I walked over a thousand miles besides those I walked at my work.

Every day in April and May the boys (regardless of age they were called boys, likewise all females were called girls) had carried mattresses out of the auditorium, a thousand more or less. I was sure I had put sheets on a million, but anyway the floor space became larger each day and the guests were arriving and it was a little too cold to sit around the outside fireplace and the evenings could be very long for those who liked to dance. When the piano was uncovered, someone said it would be fine if someone knew how to play it. Gene said she thought that I could play well enough for two-steps and waltzes, so I sent for my music. The only trouble at first was that Gene, being the only girl, complained that her feet were being danced right off her ankles.

I had known how to pick out notes in music and find the keys on the piano with one finger, then with one hand and then two, and had come close to making it sound nearly right, but it wasn't until I was fourteen and I went with a girlfriend when she had a music lesson that I heard real music. Even the scales and exercises played by that teacher sounded wonderful. I begged her to give me lessons, but of course I didn't have the seventy-five cents necessary. I said I would get an extra job, so she said yes and set a time for 11:30 the next Saturday.

I went from door to door until I found a house that had a piano and a young child around six or seven.

"Does your child play?"

"No."

"Why have a piano?" I would ask. "I'll give them fifteen-minute lessons for twenty-five cents on Saturday mornings."

I was sure I could keep ahead of their children and I finally found the three I needed, but my lessons lasted only a few weeks because the teacher found out that I had three broken fingers and that I had to play the octaves with my thumb and fourth finger on my right hand. The fact that I sometimes worked after school, or in the evenings, also Saturdays and Sundays until after midnight, made supper, and swept and dusted the house amazed her. "When would you practice?" she asked. "I expect my pupils to practice two hours a day." On and on were the many reasons why I couldn't take lessons and only one why I should, and that was because I wanted to learn to play.

It was heaven while it lasted, and I had been exposed to good music and I would never be satisfied with my kind of playing again. The teacher gave me some beginners' books, explained about time, sharps, and flats and told me to buy music and keep on trying for my own pleasure. I always loved her for her interest in me and then another good thing happened to me.

I had headed home from school one day, but I didn't need to be home before 5 because Gene worked from 7 A.M. to 7 P.M. for $1.00 a day. So I didn't need to go to work before 7 and I heard a piano being played. It came from a big house that sat a good way back from the sidewalk. There was a bush where the lawn stopped against a stone wall about two feet high. I could sit on the wall behind the bush and not be seen. I even stopped playing basketball so I could get there and hear that "somebody" practice.

Then one day I heard a violin also. For weeks, I would sit and listen but was feeling guilty, for I didn't know if I was trespassing or not. Then one day the violin stopped, the piano kept right on. Almost immediately a young man came running out of the house down the walk and turned down the sidewalk away from me; he didn't see me but I never dared to sit on that wall again.

I had heard some more good music and oh, how I hurried home to practice. I spent all my tip money for music. I even came home with a piece called "The Vamp." It had a real catchy tune, but a neighbor girl seeing it said it was bad. I used to go out and look up the street to see if anyone was coming before I dared to play it and I used to wonder how I would explain to anyone how wicked I was if I ever got caught.

The day the boys made the snowman, I saw him. I was terrified until I realized that he had never seen me and I could avoid him as much as I could. He must be wonderful to be able to play as he did.

A few days later he was talking to Mother Curry when I was passing by. She called me over and introduced him to me and finished by saying, "Laura has been playing for us to dance and I think it would be nice if you would help her. Get your violin."

"Now?" he asked, for he worked in the soda fountain.

"Yes, why not now?" she answered with a sweet smile. "The two of you can go over to the auditorium and practice playing together."

He went to get his violin and I wanted to start running. I stammered something about my unfinished tents and I knew that my face was burning; of course, she just thought I was bashful.

She said for me not to worry, she would get someone to finish for me, for me to run along that he would be there shortly.

I was seated by the piano when he came in and a waltz was open before me, so he said, "Let's try this."

When we finished he said, "Not bad."

We played a two-step.

He said, "Not bad."

Then he took a piece out of his violin case and said something about "Paree."

I shook my head.

He played it through and then said for me to try it. He said the part about the "Cows and Chickens" and "This Is the Life" had to be played just so, and he kept saying words I had never heard before. He was patient, he sang it, he danced it, he whistled it, again and again. "Quick and sharp now," he said.

We tried it over and over and I got worse and worse, my fingers couldn't go fast enough.

He said very sweetly, "You stay here and practice this, I am sure you will be better tonight."

I really tried but never knew exactly what he wanted my fingers to do.

That night he was introduced and about a hundred people on the floor clapped. We played waltzes and two-steps and then about ten o'clock he pushed that plagued piece in front of me and started playing. I let him play it through once and then I joined him. It was popular and they liked it. They started to "rag." All went well until we got to the "Cows and Chickens" and "This Is the Life" and I wasn't any better.

He stopped playing and without a word picked up his violin and walked out.

I just wanted to die. The dancers were stopped and just looking.

The tears poured down my face and I couldn't even wipe them away. I couldn't move. It seemed like hours.

Then some kind person leaned over the piano and said, "Come on, now, we like your playing better anyway."

I reached for "Moon Winks" that I knew by heart and played it. "Under a New Waterfall," someone told me later.

Everyone who had started ragging ended up in a three-step.

I had learned that talent and kindness don't always go together.

I went on playing for a week or two when again Mother Curry called to me to meet a young man, newly arrived, who played a violin.

The first thing he said was "Where did you major?"

I had never heard the word and so didn't know what he was talking about, and I am sure that my face showed I didn't.

Mother Curry mentioned his name and said, "Run along, we will forget it for now, Laura will play for us until the rest of the orchestra gets here."

A few weeks later I was only too glad to turn over the playing to the professionals and do a little dancing on my own.

The masquerades have to be told about, so why not now? The Currys gave nice prizes, and besides, people enjoyed dressing up. Gene should have been a designer for she was never happier than when getting a costume together, and she always came away with a prize.

She went to the Village and came back loaded with yards of rope. She got a galvanized wash tub from the laundry and spent all her free time unraveling the rope to the wonder of all of us. I saw her and Pinkie whispering together and figured he had something to do with the secret. He brought flattened tin cans, a rattlesnake skin, and seeds to the tent. Gene bought theatrical makeup and all of a sudden, my black cotton stockings disappeared.

When people asked her what she was doing, she would let them coax a little and then she would tell them that if they promised not to tell anyone, she would tell them. Then with a lot of whispering and giggling that she was going as September Morn and that she was going to stand in some water in the tub. Of course, it got around and even to Mrs. Curry.

Mrs. Curry came to the tent and demanded that Gene give up the idea, a big crowd was fine, but there was a limit to what one should go as.

"Why, Mrs. Curry I wouldn't do anything so terrible. You don't think I would tell anybody how I was going to dress!"

"I'm sorry, Gene. I should have known I could trust you."

Then Gene told her that she and Pinkie were going as South Sea Islanders and Pillsbury the photographer was coming up to take their pictures in front of the Indian tepee with a flashlight attachment.[8] Also, that they had made arrangements with the orchestra to play a jungle dance when they came in, and that she and Pinkie had been practicing.

Mother Curry kept their secret, and the big night arrived. All

8. This passing mention of A. C. Pillsbury is significant in that it shows the emergence of flash photography. One of Pillsbury's greatest contributions to photography was his embrace of new technologies to improve images.

went fine as planned except as they were running through the trees in the dark to the auditorium they met an old man, a guest in the camp. They jabbered something and went screaming on their way.

The next morning, as the grapevine reported, an old man who had meant to stay a few weeks came to the office and said, "I must check out. You see, I am a missionary from the South Seas and was sent back to the States for a real rest. Your pamphlets didn't say anything about natives, and what I saw last night were terrible. I had no idea that in this country—"

After being assured that the only survivor of the Yo-se-mi-ti tribe was too feeble to run through the woods and sat in front of the tepee every day, and that the ferocious creatures he had seen were only masquerade characters, he consented to stay.

Gene won a prize, a beautiful three-foot picture of Yosemite, and Pinkie won one of Vernal Falls. He gave his to her, and in time she gave both of them to me and said since they had used my stockings and had all the fun, I should have the pictures.

Pinkie had used bluing to dye his wig, and it had gotten into his hair and it wouldn't wash out; it had to be cut off as it grew out. I had blackened up, and since no one had told me to put cold cream on first, I was having trouble too. The two of us were an awesome sight for a long time.

Bill had gotten into trouble also. He had borrowed an old-fashioned bathing suit, one of those 1899 kind with a frilly cap and full gathered skirts with full bloomers underneath, puff sleeves, long black stockings and bathing slippers with ties half-way up to the knees.

On the way back from the dance we passed the swimming pool. Bill said, "What's the use of a bathing suit if you don't use it?" He ran up the stone steps to the high diving board. It was dark around the pool except for one small blob over by the bath-house door.

Pinkie and I watched for Bill to surface. We were really worried and rightly so, for Bill was fighting for his life. The cap had split as he struck the water and went over his face. The first stroke of his arms had ripped out the sleeves. The first kick had ripped apart both skirt and bloomers and they had twisted about his legs and feet. The waist was also in shreds. Before he could get to the side of the tank where he could butt his head and reach up the side, he nearly drowned.

His first words were "Never again will I condemn a girl for wearing a one-piece bathing suit." After a few more breaths he told Pinkie to go to his tent and get his robe, and he told me to beat it.

Poor old Jim, we had fixed him up as an Alaskan dance-hall dame expecting him to win a prize. He would have, too, only he never got to the auditorium. When Jim had put the corset, which we had borrowed from Sarah, on over his trousers, I had put my foot against him and really cinched him up tight. Over that had gone three borrowed petticoats, and a long black skirt, a fancy waist, and a garden hat trimmed with tiny pinecones. Then there was a liberal coating of powder and makeup, lipstick and eye shadow. It all had to wear off in time. Jim said his lungs had quit working before he got halfway across the camp. He said he had staggered back to his tent and spent the next two hours trying to get out of the steel contraption. He knew Sarah would blow her top if he cut the strings so he had wiggled and twisted until he had gotten the back to the front so he could untie the harness.

If anyone so much as pointed a finger at him he would holler and if I came around he would yell, "Get away from me, kid!"

There was another masquerade near the end of the season, after Bill had left, that nearly ended things for me. I had made up my mind to win a prize. I had borrowed an old suit of Hal's and also his shoes. Rastus had smuggled a bale of straw to the back of his tent for my use. Jim had found a sack to cover my face and someone else had found a big heavy rope for me. I cut a small breathing hole and two narrow slits for eyes. Straw stuck out of the tied cuffs and at the ankles and from under the hat and I was well padded (so I thought). I had asked a college boy whom I didn't know to help get me to the auditorium. He was to tie the rope ends around each of my arms, drag me over the ground and up the stairs (after the dance had started), drag me into the hall, then swing the looped end over the rafter and pull me up so that just the tips of the toes of the shoes touched the floor, and leave me for one dance, then come take me down and dance away with me. He did everything according to agreement except he didn't come back to take me down. I never knew his name and he would duck out of sight afterward so I never had a chance to tell him what I thought of him. I didn't dare tell any-one and point him out for fear he would get beaten up. I hope his conscience still hurts him.

I was to hang sort of limp, which I did. Someone got the idea of punching me. The idea got so popular that I was soon spin-ning, and believe me, they were really hitting. I tried to hold on till that dance was over and the boy would come take me down. I could see him out of the eye slits sitting on the sidelines talking to a girl, and he was laughing as hard as any of them at the crazy scarecrow being beat up.

I felt something warm trickling down my arms, and when I tried to move my fingers and couldn't I was sure I was bleeding to death and they had fallen off, I was sure I was going to faint. Gene had tried every trick she knew to find out what I was going as, but I had kept my secret well. I saw her dancing toward me with her partner and he was getting ready to slam me one, and I called out, "Take me down!"

I came to as I was being dragged across the floor when someone had cut the sack over my face and I heard someone say, "Why, that's a woman." I passed out again. I came to the second time lying under one of the yard faucets. The water was pouring over my face and I was strangling. I passed out again, and when I came to I was in the tent and in bed and Gene was sure mad at me. "You stick to your hiking, you can get enough attention in your own way."

Of course, I didn't go to work for several days.

The next day after the dance, Mr. Curry met Gene and said, "It was too bad Laura didn't get to the dance."

"The little fool was there, that's why she can't work today and maybe many days, she is too black and blue to move," Gene told him.

"How did she get black and blue?" he asked.

"She was the scarecrow."

"If I had known that I would have given her the prize."

"She will be glad to hear that," Gene told him.

I was, but it was my last masquerade in the Valley.

One afternoon Parsons suggested that we go over to the barn and take some pictures of his horse. When the pictures were developed, Gene had one of them with me on the horse enlarged. I had asked her why because anyone of course see that I had never been on a horse. "Just look at that horse, he has dropped his head in shame."

"Oh, it was real good of the falls," she answered.

Afterward we went to the lower meadow and crossed over the swinging bridge. It was a real scary thing to do but the boys always like to hear us scream and it gave them an excuse to carry us to the dry land on the other side.

Another night Gene and Bill and I were coming back from the Village when we heard the Glee Club Boys coming from camp. There could have been five or six or more and they usu-

White loads a donkey for firefighters, 1915. Courtesy of Yosemite National Park Archives.

ally swung along the road with arms over shoulders swaying to the rhythm of the song.

Bill said to me, "Hurry, give me your sweater." It was a "roughed-necked" style with the collar as big as the sweater, almost, and it was a dark red. We squatted in the middle of the road with the sweater over our heads. "When I start to rise up you come up slowly too," he whispered.

It was too dark to see the singers, and they were practically on top of us when Bill growled like a bear and started to rise up slowly.

The line broke and all fled but one. It happened to be the violinist. Gene went up to him and took hold of his arm. She said later that he was shaking like a leaf.

Bill grabbed Gene's arm and started running to camp. We got to the auditorium steps and collapsed in convulsions. We laughed and laughed. "They will get even, just you wait and see," Bill was able to tell us.

"You shouldn't have scared them so bad," said Gene.

"He shouldn't scare so easy. Besides, I am glad it was him who was scared so silly. It will serve him right for what he did to Laura."

"What did he do to Laura?" asked Gene in alarm.

"Walking out on her the night of the dance."

"Oh, that," she said, relieved. "She'll live."

I was taken aback because I didn't even know that Bill had known about it. I just supposed he was out climbing somewhere since he didn't dance, at least I had never seen him dance.

Could this really be the same person that had sworn to break my neck? And here he was all mad about another guy hurting my feelings and all the time I was trying to act tough and not be a blubbering baby like I thought he thought I was.

The next night was a corn feed at Happy Isles and we usually went the short way through the woods where we had to walk the planks from log to log to keep dry, for the waters had flooded most of the trail. Even with care we sometimes returned the same way, although we had to go awfully slow and feel our way along from tree to tree.

We had been all laughing about how full we were and we were all sure we had swallowed a good many wasps, saying that they got into the butter and slid right down our throats with the corn. Someone said they were so full of butter they couldn't walk a log, we had better go back by the road, and so they decided. Bill had heard about a mother bear and her two cubs hanging around Rastus's tent and said, "Let's go see if we can get a glimpse of them." Someone gave us a candle and we broke it in two and put it in our drinking cups. There being no moon, everything was pitch black.

Before we reached the meadow, our candles burned out, so we turned back and by running we caught up with the rest of

Laura and friends on a hiking break, 1915. Courtesy of Yosemite National Park Archives.

the party. Had we gone on we would have been the victims of the prank to get even, just as Bill had said they would someday.

The Glee Club Boys had slipped up the trail after we had gone over the planks to Happy Isles. They had then turned the planks and logs to lead into the deeper water. Of course, they did expect us to return that way, as we usually did. Getting wet wouldn't have bothered us too much, but being dark, somebody might have gotten lost or hurt.

Bill's tent faced the Curry end of the Happy Isles Trail and he often watched Mr. Curry as he made his rounds. On this particular morning, Bill had seen a couple of Glee Club Boys making for the trail, then came Mr. Curry. When Mr. Curry found the planks moved, he guessed the set-up and faced the boys with it.

From behind a tree Bill heard Mr. Curry tell them, "So you like to fool around with trails. Well, I have always wanted to make a good trail out of this, so after breakfast you can all come down here with picks and shovels and go to work, and I think we will build a small foot-bridge or two."

On another one of those early evening walks in late May a party of us were coming from the Village just about sundown. It was clear and cold and Parsons was walking with me. He stopped and grabbed my arm and said, "Oh, look!" He was pointing toward Glacier Point. "An icicle almost 2,000 feet or longer, don't you see it?"

The setting sun was hitting it just right, and that huge silver sliver of ice hung from the point of the overhanging rock down until it disappeared behind the trees on the Ledge Trail.

"It must have taken weeks to form that way," he said, his face beaming with the joy of discovery.

I was the only one who said I could see it. The rest just hooted and laughed. Finally, we just walked fast and got away from them.

Kidding, except by mutual consent, can be hurtful.

Parsons was quite upset. He had Indian eyes, admittedly better than the average white man's. He liked to tell tall tales and pull his share of stunts, but to lie, no. He was really hurt at their disbelief. They never let up. They would call out, "Has anyone around here seen Parsons's big icicle?" Finally, he drew away from our crowd. I sure did miss him.

A picture that I finally saw later showed three feet of snow on the overhanging rock. When it started to melt, it would form an icicle and it had no place to go but down. It would have to hang there until the sun dissolved it or the wind broke it.

Once at the breakfast table I mentioned that I guessed I had rubbed shoulders with a bear. I slept on the inside of the bed next to the side of the tent and must have been lying up against the canvas when something rubbed against me from the other side and woke me instantly. As I glanced over the covers, I saw a bear standing in the moonlight at the entrance of the tent. He was sniffing the air. Satisfied there wasn't any side of bacon to come in for, he ambled away.

At the mention of a bear soon everyone at the table had to tell of his run-in with a bear and its results. Bill reminded us again that there were bears down by the garbage dump every evening and why didn't we go down and watch them.

So one evening about fifteen of us started out after supper. Gene didn't go. "Smell garbage to see a bear! I don't want to see one that badly." I had heard her tell somebody how a bear had stomped her in 1905 when she had jumped over a log and landed on a sleeping one, surprised it had only tried to get up and away, and in the scuffle, she had been kicked. I believe she was actually afraid and I didn't blame her.

Bill explained while we were walking down the Valley about bears and their ways and everybody listened. "Garbage odors will interfere with their sense of smell, a little, but they can still hear you. Their eyes are not so good, but their speed is. And if we run into the mother bear and her two cubs, it might be just as well if we hadn't come." And then he let out one of his famous belly laughs.

It was planned that we would stretch out on the ground at arm's-length apart, not talk and be still. We had to approach against the wind. We held our noses and lay down in the grass as directed. The air at ground level was breathable. I do not know what the others were doing after that. I kept my head down. Soon it was quite dark with only the glow from the flames for light.

I thought I heard something and I raised my head slowly, enough to see through the grass that she was not thirty feet from me, coming out of the woods with her two cubs behind her. She came closer and closer, then she reared up on her hind legs and sniffed the air and growled a warning to the cubs, and they retreated to the tree line and stopped. The second time that she reared up and sniffed the air she growled. She swayed back and forth, and even I knew she was nervous. So was I.

She came to within fifteen feet when a whiff of burning meat distracted her. She must have remembered her cubs were hungry. She turned to the smoldering assortment and put out her paw and dragged a big chunk of meat toward her.

One cub had stayed at the tree line, the other had decided to follow his ma. He was right up to her before she saw him. She dropped the meat and swung out with one of her paws and hit him and he went flying through the air to land with a thud. What she must have said to him wasn't pretty either. He whimpered and went to stand with his twin.

Her domestic problem taken care of, she again turned her attention to the meat. In the fire's glow, I could see her big claws as they ripped the meat apart, and her feet stomped the heat out of it. Bill hadn't mentioned her memory, and I was hoping it was bad. She stood up again and I was sure she was thinking, "I know I saw something."

Then I wondered what the others were doing. I turned my head real slow and I looked to the right of me, there was nobody there. I turned my head to the left of me, there was nobody there. It couldn't be possible, even Bill was gone. All the things he had said not to do, they had done, including himself.

No wonder she had snorted and sniffed. She had seen something like a lot of shadows moving about the meadow. I was getting the idea that my life was not worth a plugged nickel, but fortunately her attention was divided and her cubs were hungry.

I mustn't stand up but I must put some distance between us. I watched her very carefully and every time she turned and looked at her cubs I'd push myself back a few feet. I did that until she was kind of blurry. She had called her cubs over and they were eating the cooled meat and she was watching them. I stood up and hunched over and made a dash to the nearest tree. I got behind it and stood up and peeked back to see what she was doing. Then I took off for the next tree and so on until I reached the road. Once on the road, I was willing to dare her to try and catch me.

On up the road a piece, I found the group behind a big boulder trying to decide what to do about me. "We couldn't go back to camp without you, you know, etc. etc." I had learned something from that bear. I just sniffed and let them worry about what I was thinking.

The next Sunday afternoon, Bill took his camera and said he was heading up Illilouette Canyon to take pictures of a bear that he heard was there. I guess he had to save face, and he looked a little sheepish as he passed me.[9] All I said was "Woof, woof."

We were all awaiting his return. When he came, someone called out, "Where's your camera?"

"The bear got it, and did he get some good pictures of me getting the heck out of there."

He soon had us all laughing as he told how he had crawled up and around the fallen trees and huge rocks. There isn't any trail

9. The personal camera, like Pillsbury's flashlight attachment, would have been relatively new at this time. It would have been a major purchase for a resort worker such as Pontynen, and even more so for White to have rented one. The photos would have been similarly expensive to develop or enlarge.

up that canyon. Then he came to a big old tree that had fallen. He put his camera up on the top of it first before attempting to crawl over it. He pulled himself up with the idea of jumping over when he came face to face with the biggest bear he had ever seen. "Did you ever see a man in the air headed one way, then make an about turn and go the other way?" And he roared, "Well, I did just that."

"Did you run?" someone asked.

"In that canyon? No, but I stumbled and rolled all the way down."

Someone had a real bright idea. "Laura, how about you going up to get his camera?" It was a challenge, and I went. I felt like I was being a fool. It turned out to be a hard climb and I found neither the camera nor the bear, but I'll bet he saw me because the cockles on my neck didn't stand up for nothing.

This doesn't mean that bears didn't scare me. But that came later and it was thirty years before I would tell it on myself. As I aged, I learned to laugh at the reckless, silly girl that I had been.

About fifty of the help, arms over shoulders, swayed back and forth as they stood on the porch in front of the office and looked down on the faces of the 500 or more guests and sang the Curry song as our part of the evening's entertainment. This night was a little different inasmuch as we had been practicing a parody and we weren't sure just how it would be taken. We all loved Mr. Curry, but after all he was our boss and had the power to send us all skedaddling down the hill. For many, their college tuition depended on their summer paycheck.

The parody had seemed like a good idea. As we sang we could tell that the campers liked it. But Mr. Curry was listening without any outward sign on his face as to his feelings. Again and again the audience yelled for more and still Mr. Curry stood blank-faced. Then all at once his face broke into a big smile and he started to clap with the rest of them. So we sang it again.

Then you work your bones for Curry
And you keep on working, too
And when you think you are done
There's something else for you to do.
You start in the morning,
Work late at night,
You work every minute with all your might.
You've got to be a worker
Or they'll dub you quick a shirker
They'll never treat you right.
Oh, it certainly is a fright.
For you work your bones for Curry
And you keep on working, too,
Camp Curry will certainly make it hard for you,
That's true.
And you can bet next year, I'll not be back
Working until I think my back will stack.
Camp Curry, I've certainly strained my back
And lost my mind for you.
And sleep has been a stranger, too.
They'll furnish a light
So you'll be working all night.

Mr. Curry got up on the platform and told us that "come to-morrow" we would all be treated just that way. Of course, everybody clapped and clapped. Just the same as long as the weather permitted the outdoor programs, the help were always expected to sing both the Curry song and the parody.

And all over this United States many important people will take a breath and lean back in their chairs and say, "Yes-siree, that is the way it was, I know, I was there."

As for the help, there are doctors and lawyers, teachers, scientists, and many a dignified matron who can say the same and add, "I ironed clothes, I waited tables, I made beds, I helped to sing that song many times. I was there."

The words to the real song are on the inside cover.

In Yosemite, you could stand and just look at the weather and people didn't think you were crazy. Before coming to the Valley, I had used the outdoors only to go out in and go places. Now I was out in it every day. I began to enjoy how different and how beautiful it could be.

First were the clear, cold days that really hurt your eyes, so you didn't look too much. Then came the snows that changed everything to white, and clouds of all kinds. Someone said that the clouds had all kinds of names. I never heard what they were but I liked them anyway.

A big rolling mass of clouds would start coming down Tenaya Canyon, dark and rumbling, then change its direction and slam-bang right into Clouds Rest and if it was full of water it would all fall out and come tumbling down in one big shining sheet of blue-green loveliness.

Or you would be looking at Glacier Point, with a baby-blue sky all around, and pronto, big white cottony clouds would roll over the rim and start falling as though they would fall right on you. Then a current of air would catch them and lift them again and away they would go as if to say, "Scared you, didn't I?"

Snow would be banked up on Half Dome and then a wind from the backcountry would decide to brush the Dome clean and all that powder would swoosh off at once and linger a second before beginning to fall.

In the spring after the first snow of May had turned to ice and every limb and stick and pine needle was turned into an icicle and everyone's walking was a constant crackle, at night the slightest wind would start all the pine needles to jingling just like Chinese glass chimes.

There was only one terrible sound in the mountains; I never had heard it in Yosemite and I hope that nobody ever does. And that is the roar of flames rushing through the pines.

At night on a very windy night with the thunder edging closer with every blast, and the tent flaps tied down, you knew that when it reached you it would get right in bed with you. And if your head was covered up, the lightning got in with you, too. It always ended and in the morning the world outside would look all washed and clean and good again.

One person who really loved the stormy days and roared defiance at the elements was Bill. At first, I thought him a little balmy. I really got used to him roaring out poetry, and eventually it seemed natural for him to do the unexpected. He would scream his words at the wind, and shake his fists. When a clap of thunder would answer, he would laugh and say, "I sure got him mad this time." And he would point to Half Dome and say, "That poor fellow, the one whose face is on the flat side, got mad at his wife and threw her basket at her. South Dome is her basket and she is under it. Well, they quarreled so much that when he did that old Mr. Thunder Man turned them both to stone."

How anybody could be so smart was a mystery to me. He wasn't more than four or five years older than me and yet he seemed to have read everything, could answer any question about the Valley, knew the heights of all the rocks and peaks. He loved John Muir and must have learned all his books by heart, for he would go swinging down the trail quoting what John Muir had said about this peak and that fall or just something about the Valley.

John Muir had died in the fall of 1914, and Bill said that he had died of grief. He had loved the Valley and Hetch Hetchy also and had fought the government and the cattlemen and the mining men and everyone who dared to say they were going to buy it, cut its trees, or drown it. He finally agitated until it was set aside as a park for the people. He tried to save the beauties of Hetch Hetchy but he failed and what had been a beautiful valley was turned into a reservoir for water for the people of San Francisco. He claimed there were hundreds of small canyons with little or no beauty that could have been dammed and were nearer.

Bill said it sure proved what one man could do if he got mad enough. He said that everyone should love John Muir or get out of the Valley and go back to cement sidewalks instead of enjoying the granite masterpieces. The whole wonderful Valley was a monument to his greatness. Then he would quote the lines that John Muir had written.

"Climb the mountains and get their good tidings. Nature's peace will flow into you as sunshine flows into the trees. The winds will blow their own freshness into you, and the storms their energy, while cares will drop off like autumn leaves."[10]

It took the sun quite a while to wobble its way north so that it would shine into the Valley and warm up both sides, and when it got a little north of Half Dome there it stayed until time for its journey south again.

Bill would tell me that, and then say that he was talking double talk, that the sun really stayed fairly close to one place in the big beyond and that it was the earth that was doing the jumping around and going in near circles called an orbit. That showed you went to school to find out how much you didn't know and then you ended up saying one thing when you meant the opposite.

Anyhow, I liked to think of the sun as coming up each morning, it sounded prettier than saying the earth was jumping around, and in my ignorance, I was happy. It made beautiful pictures on Mirror Lake and the tourists that knew about its magic reflections were always there with their cameras. Then after the

10. This passage comes from Muir's 1901 book titled *Our National Parks* and remains one of his most quoted writings.

*Laura overlooking Nevada Falls and Half Dome, 1915. Courtesy of
Yosemite National Park Archives.*

pictures were printed, you didn't know which way was up. The
swimming pool at Curry's was the same way.

Mirror Lake was a wonderful place to spend an early morning. The double picture of Mount Watkins and Clouds Rest and
Washington's Column, the birds singing their hearts out, and
the chipmunks begging bread crumbs, and the smell of the pines
and the far-awayness of the world. Well, you would never forget it.

Once I had shown an interest in Indian names, and Bill made
sort of a game of it. He would paint to a certain rock formation

and call out its Indian name and I was supposed to answer and in that way learn to name it.

If we were in the upper part of the Valley, he would point first to Half Dome, and I would answer quickly for I knew that one, Tis-se-yek, then he would swing around and point or call out Vernal Falls, meaning white water—I would call back Pai-war-ah, then came Glacier Point and I'd hesitate and he would say "One black mark for you" and tell me again it was Pa-tell-ima. If we were at the other end and he took a spell of being teacher of Indian he would point to El Capitan and I liked it so I knew it was Tu-Took-ah-nulsh. "What did the Indians call themselves? Meaning children of light?" I knew that one, Ah-wah-nee-chees, and the Valley they called Ah-wah-nee meaning deep grassy vale. Then he would laugh and say I would be graduating real soon, and I would tell him that the Piutes called the Valley U-zer-mai-ti and from that the soldiers thought it sounded like Yo-sem-i-tee and now we call it Yosemite.

Another game he had, I always let him win. If we were on our way to the Village he would say, "I'll buy you a soda, if you lose, you get a cornucopia." He needed his money for college, so I always let him win. Besides, the cones were good and you could always eat the container.

"Come to Berkeley and I will take you up Mt. Tamalpais," he might say. Well, I might as well have had a soda, for he never got to college and I never got on top of Mt. Tamalpais. So much for kid dreaming.

One of our early trips was to Clouds Rest. On the top we sat and looked. Out there to the north was a place called Hetch Hetchy and Tenaya Canyon, and off to the east was the high country unknown to me; Mount Dana, and Starr King, is where Bill and his friends Will and Pinkie were going for a week with a pack burro. Bill was going to map out his route in his attempt to climb Mount Starr King later in the summer.

"You'll be along, because we have decided to name the burro after you."

"Why?"

"Oh, he has the same trick of stopping for breath but pretending he is looking at the scenery."

I told him I had to ask questions because it was all so new to me.

He was nice about it, said to ask all the questions I wanted to, said he was the same way the first time he came up, and then he went home and read every book he could find on the subject and each year he learned more and more.

Bill said, pointing to the east, "Over there is a good trip, to Merced Lake. If we could start out Saturday night and walk all night." We did just that later in the season with near fatal results for the other girl in the party.

Directly south was Half Dome, the most famous Dome in the world, and no matter from what angle you looked at it, it was different. Probably the most photographed piece of granite in the Valley. If I could have been able to read minds at that time I would have seen an idea growing.

Glacier Point was another place I must go. And on down the Pohona Trail, meaning in Indian Puffing Wind, but I mustn't go until the mariposa lilies were in bloom, and to be sure to take a camera, for the light was just right when you reached the Inspiration Point for pictures of the Valley and also Bridal Veil Falls further on down the trail. "You will never forget it," he said.

The sun was going down behind El Capitan at the west of the Valley and I would never be so high again. The bite of the air was exhilarating. The blocks of granite that were stacked up and looked like a pyramid, looked smooth from the Valley. Of course, they hadn't been stacked up there at all. Bill had explained when we arrived, that it was the result of the glacier that had ground its way down Tenaya Canyon, that had frozen around the west slope and cracked the granite, and would have pushed the huge slabs into the Valley if the glacier had not melted when it did. Some of the rocks had let loose anyway after a few thousand earthquakes and he had asked me how I would have liked the Valley when it was a big lake, several million years ago. It was all too much for me, I much preferred to accept the beauty that resulted and be glad I lived now and was able to see it.

Bill stood up and stretched and called out, "Oh the beauty I have seen that Valley folks never know" and then laughed, "It is a crime to remember such lovely lines, and not the name of the person who wrote them."

It was time to start the long eleven miles back to camp. For once more there was a trip that had not turned out a near disaster, just memories and a few blisters.

It was about the same time of the early spring, that we took a trip to look at Bridal Veil Falls and it was especially beautiful because of the heavy snow run-off. Bill said that John Muir had written about this fall having a difference from the rest of the falls. Where the others had to cut their way through the granite at the top, Bridal Veil after coming down a sloped piece of granite at a terrific speed just jumped out away from the wall, and if you stood at a certain place on the north of the falls you could see the sky.

Reaching the falls, Bill climbed and reclimbed the left sidewall but he could not find the right place. "Everything had got to be just right to find the unusual things," he said.

I don't know who suggested it, but we went behind the fall and had a picture taken. The camera was as soaked as the rest of us, what a beating those cameras took, but the pictures turned out really good. It was a crazy thing to do because big boulders and sometimes large logs came down with the falls. Had one of them hit us on the head I am sure no ranger would have thought to look behind a fall for a crazy bunch of kids (two girls were along with us).

It was after the snows had left the floor of the Valley and also the rim when somebody showed Bill a picture of several feet of snow, supposedly in a box canyon in Tenaya Canyon where they said it never melted.

There was no trail to follow once you had left the Zig Zags Trail and headed down into the canyon. We piled rocks so that we would find our way back again. We even lugged a limb along to use as a ladder. There was seldom a level spot to set your feet.

We found a very dangerous spot and were glad we had come upon it in the daylight. Big holes that had been ground out by the force of water against granite boulders were large enough to have swallowed us up entirely. There were many smaller holes in the process of the making. Probably a granite boulder resting in a hollow spot to start with, and water started whirling the rock around and around and digging deeper and deeper year after year.

Being a girl, I had another theory. I imagined that it was a place where the Indian women came to grind their corn into meal, and that when the soldiers came, they had panicked and left their grinding rock. Well, Bill thought that very funny and said the grinding rock that had made the biggest hole must have been owned by a double giant with a hand as big as a scoop shovel, said I must be hungry to have even thought of such a thing. Anyhow, someday a scientist with a good camera will run across them and write a big article about them, and people will start breaking their necks getting to see the curiosities. Anyway, seeing them first doesn't make us a Balboa or a Columbus, but we did get a little of the feeling of discovery.

We went way beyond these holes but didn't find the ice cave, and decided we had better get out while we had light to walk by, so we retraced our steps and followed the rock pile markers we had left and had no difficulty finding our way out.

The trip was without incident other than the nice feeling that maybe we had walked in strange places and found something of interest.

The 3rd of July was a Sunday, and Bill came up to me and asked, "Want to go on a hike?"

"Sure, where to?"

"Indian Canyon. See if you can get a sandwich or something from the kitchen."

I hurried over to the kitchen, everyone was gone but the scrub boy and he didn't know where things were. I found bread and a jar of jelly and made two sandwiches and also picked up two lemons.

On my way back to the tent, I ran into Gene, who was talking to Jim. I said, "I am going to take a little hike with Bill to Indian Canyon."

"Where in the world is that?" she asked. "Can't you stay in camp once in a while?"

Jim said, "For goodness' sake, let the kid go, I've been up there many times myself."

Gene didn't want any of the boys to think ill of her so she nodded and I took off to get my khaki divided skirt and middie. Then I took out across the meadow the big oak tree where Bill had said to meet him.

As I passed the tent where my Great-Aunt was staying for the summer, I waved to her. She watched me run over to where Bill was waiting and saw him pick up a long coil of rope and sling it over his shoulder. He took the bag with the sandwiches and tied it to his belt, and we started toward the Arches.

"Where is Indian Canyon?" I asked.

"Just east of the Yosemite Falls. The Indians used it to enter and leave the Valley. You see, they never built bridges and when the river was high it was too dangerous to swim. John Muir wrote of coming down it one time, but I never heard of a white person climbing up and out of the Valley by that route. There was a waterfall on the right side of the canyon called Lehamite, meaning place where the arrow wood grows. I think that after so many years the Indian trail must be washed away, but I thought we might find something left of it."

We came to a lot of loose rocks and Bill said he thought we were at the base of the slide. So we began to work our way up and over the boulders. The rocks were usually so smooth and so large that there were no handholds, and Bill would have to work his way on top and throw me the end of the rope, then I would scramble up and there was always another one in front of us.

Bill had not brought his watch, but he was sure we had been climbing an hour and said that certainly we should have been near the top by now.

We went on climbing over boulders and up and around projections for what he thought was another hour. He looked at the descending sun and said he guessed he had missed the main part of the canyon. "We have come over places that we just can't go back to, there is no place to tie a rope." For the first time, I saw him worried about a climb.

Finally, he pulled himself up and over a projection and let out a loud whistle. "We're not anywhere near the place we should be."

When I had reached him, he pointed to the west. "There is the slide I wanted to climb. We were climbing up the bed of that old fall Lehamite. No wonder we can't make any time."

He had me stay where I was and he took the rope and backtracked, trying to find a way into the canyon or another route up the wall. I couldn't see him but I heard a great deal of falling rocks. I certainly wouldn't have known how to go up or down. I waited for what seemed like a long time and the only comfort I had was that while there were falling rocks to hear he must be alive.

Finally, he appeared and said there just wasn't any other way for us to go but up the waterfall route.

"Have you ever climbed a chimney?"

"You mean one of those things that smoke comes out of?"

"No, this is of rock, and what comes out of it is blisters."

Up ahead of us was a boulder that looked as though an earthquake had split it in two. It was just wide enough for a person to squeeze into at the bottom. Bill went over and looked up through the opening for several minutes. "It is about the same opening clear to the top. We can climb it if we don't get too tired before getting to the top. If I can make it up there, I can let down the rope and you will just have to keep climbing till you get to it."

He stood and looked at me for a few minutes. "To climb a chimney, you squeeze in and put your arms out and get a good suction with the palms of your hands, brace your shoulders, pull your legs up and try and get a good suction with the soles of your feet against your shoes. That is a spread eagle. Then relax your arms and shoulders and inch up as far as you can and brace them again, pull up your legs and get another foothold. Repeat this to the top or until you reach the rope. If once you let go, all of you will shoot right back to the bottom."

I wanted to ask him if he thought he could drag me up by my neck but one look at his face showed me that he was really worried and had no time for kidding.

He took one of the sandwiches out of the bag and divided it and gave me one lemon and said not to throw away the rind. "There won't be any water until we reach Mirror Lake. That daylight is going fast." He put the other sandwich in his pocket.

I watched him squeeze into the opening and spread eagle and it didn't look too difficult. However, I did find that my muscles were not as good as his. I was plenty tired before I ever got to the rope. I just had to make it. Finally, I reached out and got a good grip over the knot that he had tied in the end of it. He didn't exactly pull me up the rest of the way, but the rope did make it much easier. I knew I was cut in places before I had reached the top and my feet were out of my tennis shoes and hurting terribly.

At the top, I swung around and sat on the big boulder beside him and we both looked at the tops of my tennis shoes dangling from my ankles. The bottoms were gone. "You might as well throw them away, you can't walk in them." So I tossed them away as we stood up to see what was next.

Bill was looking at the sun just disappearing over El Capitan.

"One more hour of light and we are not at the top yet. The light is already gone from the Valley, we had better get going."

My throat was full of granite dust and my tongue was swollen. I had lost count of bruises and rock scratches. The khaki skirt had been a nuisance but it had also saved me some bad cuts.

"Here, take this," Bill said, handing me a small, smooth pebble. "It's too big to swallow and it will help keep the saliva working and will keep your mouth from stiffening.

"Lincoln once said, "This too will pass." Let's prove he was right."

"Didn't you tell me that he had given us this Valley?"

"Yes, in a way. He as president had the power to turn it over to the people to enjoy and care for, but we as the people of California gave him the gold that helped him win the Civil War, so we gained by it. But let us get going or we are not going to gain anything." He grabbed my hand and we started up again.

At last I felt pine needles under my feet, and how good it felt. I wanted to rest my feet but Bill said, "I smell water." And he started pulling me toward North Dome.

We could still see a little and without realizing it we angled off to the right and were going downhill. We were above the Arches, in sort of a small depression and when we reached the little creek we jumped off a rock and fell onto the cool, wet bank. Fortunately, we didn't break a leg, one more bump didn't make much difference to me. But it did bring Bill to his senses.

"For an experienced hiker, I've done everything wrong today. I'm starting right now to remember a few things. Don't you dare fill up with that cold water. Lie on your stomach and let your

White on a break by a creek, 1915. Courtesy of Yosemite National Park Archives.

wrists soak up the cold water until you feel rested. Then scoop up a little to put in your mouth, don't swallow it, just hold it and then spit it out. It will wash out some of the gravel dust instead of down into your throat. Then take a swallow, wash your face and rest some more."

He looked down at the camp below us. "It's too bad we are not birds, we could take off and be there in a few minutes. We were in too much of a hurry to get to water. Now we will have to retrace our steps and climb back up out of this place."

"How did you know there was water here?" I asked. "There is no waterfall coming over the Arches anymore."

"Botany," he grinned. "If there were no water, there would be no moss. And the moss is dark, which means that it is wet. I just remembered that the dark spots were still on the Arches."

Then Bill added, "We are rested, we have had our water. Somewhere above us is a trail, let's go and find it."

Off we went holding hands feeling around in the dark. It was slippery and we began to run into brush. Finally, my feet felt the softness of the fine pulverized needles of the trail.

"Thank you, mules," I said as my sore feet were cushioned by trampled needles. We turned east toward North Dome and Tenaya Canyon.

When we reached the sign, Bill sat down under it and said, "I've sure pulled some boners on this trip. First I was sure that when you saw the rope you would back down. Second, I didn't scout around enough to make sure I had the right start. And even though we are not supposed to make a fire, I usually carry a few matches anyway. Today, I didn't. I should have brought a canteen, and I didn't. Anyhow, we should be back in camp in a few hours and it will be all downhill."

Then he made the biggest mistake of all, he walked around the sign. And being too dark to read it, he just went off to the left thinking we were headed toward the Zig Zags.

After a while Bill said, "We are going uphill instead of down. We are walking into too much brush. And occasionally we come to a fallen tree. I believe we are lost."

"I'm cold," I said through chattering teeth.

"Of course you are, you are all of seven or eight thousand feet up with the air off of thirteen glaciers blowing right at you."

I was so tired I didn't care who made records, he could make them all. I wanted to rest. And he wouldn't let me. Finally, we came to a big tree across the trail and he said for me to sit down till he could find out where the trail continued. "I'll have to find a tree blaze, the chips in the bark, about five feet up that the rangers make so they can find their way when the snows are deep."

I sat down. When he had found a blaze, he would call out and I would find him by his voice. Then he would go off in the dark again to find the next one.

My hair was down, all the hairpins had been lost somewhere. My hands were full of pitch from feeling around for blazes. Khaki is tight woven and the skirt came to my ankles. And when I sat down, I could wrap it around my feet and that helped some. Bill had on cords and a sleeveless undershirt and heavy hiking boots. I was sure he was cold too.

We must have stumbled around for four or five hours. When the moon came up, it came up fiery red and was pointed. In a few minutes, it shaped into a half moon without much light. We made better time. We seemed to be up above the trees, and what trees we saw looked white. Bill said that we must be in an aspen grove. He said that sometime there must have been a forest fire that burned off the pines. The first trees to take root on a "burn" were aspens because their seeds are lighter and the wind carries them easier.

The moonlight did something else, it showed me who my company was. I had felt the presence of something several times when sitting by a tree waiting for Bill to call out to me. With the light, I could see the bear. He probably had never seen anything like me. I couldn't have run, and where would I have run to? I didn't know where I was. Bill said that sooner or later we would connect up with another trail. That of course was a comforting thought.

Well, I followed Bill, and the bear followed me, and finally we did hit another trail, but no signs. Bill was so happy he felt silly, so he started the old kid rhyme used to choose sides.

Eenie, minnie, mo
Opoluchi, popaluchi,
I take you.

Since his arm was pointing left that was the way we went. The trail widened and we came to a flat place. He started pulling me up and down the trail until I yelled stop. "Well, I'll bet I got a little circulation built up."

Somewhere before we had hit the real trail we had come to a creek, and not knowing how deep it was, Bill had tied the rope around his waist giving me the other end. It must have been about three feet deep. So he said he would carry me over because khaki dried slowly and would make me colder.

When he let me down I asked, "Do bears swim?"

Bill just stared. "Did you see him, too?"

I nodded.

"I've been scared to death you would see him and panic," he mumbled.

I said, "I've faced bears before, and I wasn't the one who ran."

"I know I acted badly that trip, and I will have to live with that fact all my life," he said very slowly. "But right now I am trying to get you back to camp all in one piece. Can't you forget and maybe forgive?"

I nodded, feeling quite ashamed of myself, and we started on again.

We were making good time after we had hit the good trail. Then Bill saw a big black space in front of him. "Golly, I bet we have reached Hetch Hetchy." He took the rope and tied it around his waist and then put a couple of loops around a small tree and gave me the end. "Play this out to me if I call out." So he went off in the semidarkness and I was left alone again, but this time no bear.

Soon he called out to me, "Tie the rope and follow it to where I am." Which I did. Bill was laughing when I reached him and I soon saw why and joined him.

"We have done what hundreds of lost people have done, we have walked in a circle." He pointed east to where we had come up out of the canyon, and now we were on the west side of Indian Canyon. Now that we knew where we were it would be a simple matter to go west to Yosemite Falls then downhill all the way to the Valley. We didn't stop, not even when we had to go through the mists, and got wet all over, until we reached the Yosemite Falls Camp, where we flopped into a couple of reclining camp chairs.

Bill jumped up as though he had sat on some ants.

"Hey! Look what I found," he cried out as he pulled a dirty sack with a wet, soggy sandwich out of his hip pocket and broke it in half. A sandwich never tasted better.

Daylight was just breaking.

Back at camp, when we had failed to show up, Gene had hunted up Jim and asked him where Indian Canyon was.

He admitted that he didn't know where it was, that he just wanted to see me have a good time. Of course, the camp was concerned. The rangers were called in and said there was no trail up Indian Canyon, and if we had attempted it, we were probably on a ledge somewhere and when daylight came they would try and find us.

Gene thought of Auntie, and they went to question her and found out about the rope.

Three searching parties were decided upon. One would go up Tenaya Canyon, one up Yosemite Falls Trail and one would go with the rangers to Indian Canyon, where they had found loose rocks we had caused to fall so they knew where to start.

Mr. Curry said no one was to leave camp until daylight. He then told Mrs. Curry to see that Gene got some rest. Mother Curry sent one of the other women to see that Gene went to bed, which she did, but as soon as the woman was asleep, she got up and dressed and roamed the Valley again. To my face, if I would ask her about breaking my neck, she would say, "If you break it, it is your neck." What she said and what she meant were never the same.

That was how it came about that she was the first to see us coming up the road, about a block from the main entrance. She ran forward and grabbed Bill behind his neck with one hand and me with the other and we were jerked and pushed into camp. We were too tired to raise a finger and she was talking a blue streak.

When my head stopped bobbing, I opened my eyes and there stood Mother Curry in a bathrobe and her white hair falling to her waist, and I thought she looked like an angel.

"You poor dears" were her first words. "Gene, stop shaking her, can't you see that the child is near dead. Get her cleaned up and put her to bed. I'll see that a nice breakfast is sent down for both of them."

"Not me, Mother Curry," spoke up Bill. "A good bath and I'm ready to compete in the swimming contest this afternoon. I made so many wrong calculations on that trip, so now I'll have to win the match to show you I am sorry for all this trouble."

Mrs. Curry smiled and told him, "Thank you for getting her back."

Mr. Curry was gruffer. "When you kids are able, I want to see both of you in my office."

The rescue parties had spotted us and a cheer went up. "The kids are back! The kids are back!"

I woke up to a lot of cheering. Yes, the Fourth of July (1915) and the races were on. I was supposed to have been in them but not with the kind of feet I had. Someone had said that the ranger had said that I had walked thirty-five miles with my bare feet. I turned over and went back to sleep.

A few days later, Bill and I stood before Mr. Curry and he said we could not go out of camp at any time without his permission.

"Why didn't you light a fire and wait until daylight to come?"

Bill actually hung his head. "Sir, I didn't take any matches."

"Don't ever go out of camp without matches again."

"I won't, sir."

"Anymore hikes you take someone along so they can come back and tell me where you crazy kids are."

And Bill said, "Yes, sir."

Life became unbearable, we went to the office a few days later and asked if we could go to the Village for an ice-cream cone.

"What's the matter with my ice-cream cones?"

"The soda-jerks are the ones we scared that night," I spoke up.

Mr. Curry grinned and said, "Run along. How long do you expect to be gone?"

"Maybe an hour."

And so it went, bored with having to stay in camp. I walked up to a new lifeguard at the pool and said, "What do you do when someone is drowning?"

"Jump into the deep end and yell help and I'll show you."

I yelled, "Help! Help!" And he showed me by throwing me a life-preserver ring that hit me on my head and knocked me out.

When I came to he was standing over me, with a big grin. "Are you satisfied now?"

I went to my tent and took a mirror and looked at the big goose egg on the top of my head.

Once with permission and Pinkie's protection, we went to the foot of Yosemite Falls. There were plenty of big rocks, but just thinking of all the peaks that needed climbing made us glum. Bill was waxing a string to put in a can to make a Lion Roarer. "Somewhere I read that this ought to work," he said and then he pulled the string. It worked.

I sprang up and started to run over the top of the boulders. Free at last, and it was catching. The two boys took out after me, we took some terrible leaps.

Pinkie yelled, "Look at that girl go. I believe she is Pearl White."[11]

I yelled back, "I thought you would never guess it."

The *Perils of Pauline* was a very popular movie serial at the time in which the heroine was always getting nearly killed and she dared everything dangerous.

On the way back to camp, Bill was having lots of fun making the Lion roar. The next morning when I went to care for my tents I found one of my renters almost sick with fear. The dresser had been dragged in front of the tent opening along with the wash stand and chair and the tent flaps were tied. What a miserable night she must have spent. I had quite a time getting in to her.

"If I had known they had lions in the Valley, I never would have come up here alone."

I had to tell her about the can with the rosin strings and that our mountain lions preferred deer meat to humans, and that

---

11. Pearl White was an early star of stage and screen who played the titular role in *The Perils of Pauline*.

Laura overlooking Nevada Falls, 1915. Courtesy of Yosemite National Park Archives.

they preferred to live further back in the mountains. Of course, I hoped I was right. I finally had her feeling better, and she got up and dressed and went to breakfast. I told Bill, and of course he put the can away.

The next Sunday Bill disappeared early, at least he didn't come to breakfast. He was eating at our table now. Willie of his old hiking days came up and asked me if I knew where Bill was, I told him that I supposed Bill was with him. Will had avoided me most of the time and I felt that he disliked me for taking Bill away from him. I was sorry that I seemed to have broken up a friendship. Will later in the season even followed us to Lake Merced, so I guess he didn't hate me too much.

The following Saturday evening Bill said, "How would you like to go to Half Dome?" I supposed he meant just to follow the original trail to the foot of the Dome where the rope had been. "I got permission from Curry for the trip if Pinkie goes along. All he asked me was 'Is it someplace someone else has been?'" Here Bill started to laugh. "I didn't tell him that it was back in 1875. Better be ready to leave by four in the morning, it will be eleven miles each way, plus." He didn't say what that plus meant.

I thought that if Mr. Curry had given his consent, then of course Gene couldn't say no. I waited until she was almost asleep and I said, kinda low, "Mr. Curry said we could go on a hike tomorrow."

"It's all right with me. I can't see how you could do worse than you did last time." And she turned over and went back to sleep.

I set the alarm and put it under my pillow, and at the first ring I snapped it off and got up to dress.

I wore a straight skirt and it was a little shorter than the divided skirt and not so bulky, and I had a new pair of tennis shoes. I took two blanket pins and put them in my pocket. I intended to see where I was going after this, rather than flapping skirts hiding my feet.

The three of us made good time in the beauty of breaking day and passed Happy Isles in quick time. If you don't want to get wet, or if you are riding a horse, you have to take the long trail that angles off the end up to Glacier Point. But before you get there, a trail went off to the left and came back to join the regular trail above or below Nevada Falls. I had never taken it.

We took the short trail that went to the foot of Vernal Falls then up the rock steps that someone had chiseled out of the granite. There was no railing there in those days, it was slippery because it was always wet, and the mists blew over you every step of the way.

Once out of the mist, and especially so early in the morning, it was quite cold, but Bill said keep moving, which we did. We passed the Emerald Pool and Silver Apron and Bill said that beautiful green sheet of water could wash you off your feet it was so powerful, even if it was quiet, a warning that I remembered on another hike.

We went up the Zig Zags to a side path to Nevada Falls and stood on the "jitter rock" and laughed at the trembling and watched the fall gush out beneath us. It was the noisiest fall in the Valley.

We turned off onto the Clouds Rest Trail and after several miles made another left-hand turn toward the base of the north side of Half Dome. From there, it was a new trail to me.

When we reached the saddle, Bill said, "Do me a favor?"

"Sure."

"Let me blindfold your eyes."

So I let him tie his big handkerchief over my eyes. With Bill on one side and Pinkie on the other, I was led up and over the saddle to the base of the Dome. The blindfold was taken off. I was standing at the foot of the 600-foot climb. It looked straight up. I looked up at that naked granite with a knotted clothesline dangling from a few eyebolts.

I wanted to say, "What's the matter with you boys? I am not a bird." But when I turned around I saw Bill wink at Pinkie. That decided me. I said, "When do we start?" Bill let out a whoop.

Pinkie asked him who helped him put up the rope.

"Nobody did, I came up here by myself last Sunday, and by going barefooted, reached the first eyebolt, attached the rope and made a try for the second one. I was sure glad to find that I had enough rope to reach the top eyebolt. I have been helping myself to every piece of dangling rope in camp. It's just clothesline and will hold one of us at a time. It better hold. I didn't bring any lunch. If we don't make it, a lunch won't do us any good. If we do make it, why, what's a lunch compared to glory?"

"How are you going to put a shirt up there, you haven't any left?" I asked.

"Oh, I borrowed a sheet from Camp Curry. A shirt wouldn't be seen." He laughed.

"What if I don't make it?" I asked, busy pinning up my skirt. I wasn't old enough to be a lady, and I wasn't going to climb any more rocks and not see what my feet were doing.

"Well, I guess you will have the grandest headstone of anybody in the world," he answered.

Pinkie reminded Bill that he promised Curry to follow us, not lead us, or to go everywhere we went. If we did anything crazy, he was to come back and report it. "I think you are doing something mighty dern crazy right now."

As Bill started to go up the rope he yelled back for Pinkie to follow me so he could catch me if I fell.

Pinkie turned to me and said, with a weak smile, "Who's going to catch me?"

I grinned back, not knowing how to answer that question.

"I don't see why a couple of guys have to break their necks over you?" He was grinning, so I guessed he wasn't really sore about it.

I was amazed to see how much the Dome resembled an onion. It seemed to be in layers, only the peelings were granite, and what had appeared so smooth from the Valley looked like piled-up rocks, especially one side of the front.

Bill had reached a small three-inch ledge and he called to me to come on. I didn't have any trouble reaching him, and being lighter than he was I hadn't worried about the rope breaking. When I reached the ledge, he let go of the rope and when I got opposite to him, he took my picture, then told me to go on up. I wasn't scared and had no trouble reaching the top.

The boys took pictures of each other and then came on up.

We dug around in a rock mound and found an old tin can, and

Laura on the Clothes-Line Route, 1915. Courtesy of Yosemite National Park Archives.

Bill on the Clothes-Line Route, 1915. Courtesy of Yosemite National Park Archives.

Laura on Half Dome, 1915. Courtesy of Yosemite National Park Archives.

Laura, Bill, and friend on Half Dome's subdome, 1915. Courtesy of Yosemite National Park Archives.

in it was someone's name and the date. It was 1875, the name was so faded we couldn't make it out. We signed our names and the date and put the old yellow paper back into the can, piled the rocks over it again and went to see what else there was.

The overhanging rock was not natural: someone had pushed it partly over the edge. I went out on it seven times, standing, and the last time lost my balance, getting back in just enough time to give me a good scare. I wouldn't stand up again. I had lost my nerve. For years I used to have an occasional nightmare and I was always falling and falling. I never ever landed. Bill had climbed quite a way down the front to take pictures and they were unusual.

There was little else to do except watch Bill get the sheet ready. He tied pieces of rope to two corners and weighted the other two corners with small rocks before he slung it over the side. Either the knots were tied too weakly or the rocks were too heavy, for it jerked from his hands and went plunging to the bottom. It was then that Bill noticed the groups of people back at camp.

"Look at those people, I'll bet every telescope in camp is trained on us."

They were, and we had been fired. Some people had heard the whistle made by the sheet going through the air and said it was me and they had heard me scream.

We started south across the top of the Dome, for Bill was sure that we could slide down and come out at Eagle's Point. Pinkie went about halfway and sat down on a cut-out place on the top of the Dome, called a lip, at least that is what I called it. We took his picture, the only one of its kind in the world.

Maybe we could have found a way down as Bill thought if we had been nearer the face of the Dome, but from where we were, we were soon unable to stand upright. We slid around on our seats, looking for a crevice, but finally had to give up and crawl back up again on our hands and knees. The drop was too straight and not a handhold in sight, and one more wiggle and over we would have gone.

When we got back to the north side, Bill said for me to go first and not to look back. "If the rope breaks with you, we will have to fly back."

I disobeyed and looked back even though I had been told that once over the hump I couldn't see them anyway. I slipped and split my elbow. I regained my footing and continued on down. I knew that when Bill saw the blood he would be furious. When he came down he sure did say plenty about girls not being able to follow orders, that one had to think of the other fellows' safety and be dependable. All of it was true, but I just had to say something, so I said, "It's not the first rocks I've left my blood on, and it probably won't be the last." Which also proved to be true.

Once down, Bill sprung another surprise. "I'll take you home the way I went last Sunday. Why waste time on all those miles when we can sit down and whiz whiz be down there close to Nevada Falls." So he sat down, grabbed his knees, and went whizzing away, leaning this way and that to keep from hitting projecting rocks or stumps or trees.

"I'll bet those pine needles hadn't been disturbed since they had been falling over the centuries till Bill showed up," I said.

Pinkie shook his head and said, "I'm not going to walk all those miles by myself, and Curry said to follow, so here goes." Before he sat down, he looked at me and said, "You and your fancy pants might not do so well."

He was right, my fancy pants did not do so well. The loose folds acted like a scoop and packed the pine needles in until I looked like a fat lady in a circus. When I reached the bottom, I had to shake like a dog to be able to walk, and worst of all a good many had kept going after they had reached me. Later I was sure teased because I had to stand up to eat. Only the boys knew what had happened to me. Eventually the needles must have dissolved.

We had saved miles, and being hungry, we made good time on the way back. I had unpinned my skirts and I had resolved that, lady or not, by the next time I saw Yosemite I would have a pair of hiking breeches. I had seen a few guests wearing them.

It was late when we reached camp and we had no idea what we had started.

Gene was getting used to scares, and just looked at me.

Mr. Curry said, "I fired the three of you, but now that you are safely back I'll rehire you. I shouldn't have to pay insurance on dern fools."

When our pictures were developed, they were a sensation. They passed from hand to hand until they were nearly worn out. Everyone seemed to want to go to the top of the Dome. A trip was planned for the next Sunday, and Mr. Pillsbury agreed to take his moving pictures camera and go with them to take pictures of them climbing around the Dome. We had to stay in camp. We had had our day of glory. About twenty college boys and girls made the second trip.

Don Tresidder had gone up with a bigger, stronger rope and replaced the clothesline we had gone up on.

Mr. Curry toured the state that winter with the pictures of their climb. And I went to see them when he was in Los Angeles. Afterward, I went up to him and said, "You ought to be ashamed of yourself. Not one word about Bill, who made the taking of those pictures possible."

He pulled his mustache and grinned, "Why should I? He stole my tent and ropes to do it."

"Mr. Curry," I answered, "the sons and daughters of your friends do not steal."

"You're right." And we had a good laugh.

That was the last time I saw him, for he passed away before the next season. Camp Curry was never the same again, at least some of the old timers have reported.

I doubt if Bill ever gave any thought to the glory. He had his eyes on other climbs and other problems in life to conquer.

Gene was really the only casualty indirectly resulting from our trip. When the pictures were developed, Bill came running all the way from the Village to show them to me, although Jungle Town was off limits, he came tearing down to our tent and we were sitting on the trunk looking at the pictures and oohing and ahing over them when Gene came in, and she didn't like seeing him there and told him so. He didn't move.

"Get out, Bill," she said crossly. "I want to go to bed."

"O.K., Gene. Just a minute, we have only a couple more to look at."

She said, "Go now, if you don't, I'm going to start to undress."

He jumped off the trunk and said, "I always liked you, but I never thought you were that kind of woman." And he ran from the tent.

Gene had gotten into bed and I was looking over the pictures again when Bill came back into the tent with a dynamite box under his arm. He put it up by the head of the bed and knelt down, and lighted the fuse, talking all the time.

I sat and watched him, never realizing that it might be dangerous, and I think Gene was equally fascinated.

When the fuse was only an inch long he let out a whoop and then yelled, "Good-bye, Gene." And dashed from the tent.

Almost instantly Gene was out of bed and without thinking she hauled off and kicked the box. She let out an awful scream and ordered me to get that thing out of there. "Throw it into the meadow before it goes off," she screamed at me a couple of times.

I grabbed it, and started across the road with it. It was a bright moonlight night, and as I ran from the tent I saw a woman and two children coming down the road. She saw the smoking box and must have read the word "Dynamite" on the box, for she grabbed the children and ran. I don't think the kids' feet touched the ground.

I threw the box into the meadow. The fuse was even with the box. It went out. And nothing happened.

I heard Bill laughing, and Gene was telling him that he had better never let her see him again.

Bill didn't show up at our table, and he told me that the cook was letting him eat in the kitchen.

About a week later he said, "I just can't stand Gene being mad at me. Come on, and let's go to the Village and see if I can't find a peace offering for her."

He picked out a beautiful hand-colored picture of the entrance to the Valley. I thought of all the cones I had eaten to save his money, and there it went, to another girl. That was the way of life sometimes. Then of course Gene did deserve something, and he had to ease his conscience some way.

We went back and waited in the meadow until Gene came down to the tent. Bill unwrapped the picture and went and stood at the entrance of the tent and said over and over, "Please, please."

Gene gave in and hugged him, oohed and ahed about the beauty of the picture. I fell heir to it in time and I love it, too.

Bill returned to eat at our table and there was peace again for a while.

Jungle Town (the help's quarters) had been completed with the girls given tents facing the road, the boys the end tents and the row of tents that faced the pool.

The tent behind us had a boy in it who just didn't fit in with plans. He wouldn't go on a walk, or mix with anyone, and was so out of place in the mountains. No khakis for him, he was always dressed up in a suit and very fancy ties. Those ties became the talk of the other boys and got on their nerves. He would stalk by without a word, and I would hear some boy remark, "That tie, it has to go."

"Things might happen back at your tent tonight," Bill whispered to me as we left the table. It did, and I was several days getting the awful mix-up straightened out. I questioned all the boys and seems like most of them were in it, but knew only their part, but I finally got the start of it.

A rope had been coiled loosely under the covers around the cot, Bill had been planted under the cot to wait until our "tie man" had gotten asleep. The boy was known to undress down to his BVDs in the dark. The boys involved had planned to tie him up and carry him to the pool and duck him until he would promise not to wear a tie in camp.

Nothing went as planned. Awakened, he discovered the rope and someone under his bed. Bill had an awful time getting free of the ropes, free of the fists of the boy, and of the tent. Once in the clear he had taken off on a run with the boy after him. Bill raced to the Campfire Circle, the boy in hot pursuit, they had circled the fire several times to the whooping of the guests before the boy realized that he was in his BVDs. He dashed back to his tent.

The rest of the boys spread out on the ground in the dark and watched him as he rewound the rope and climbed the tree in front of his tent. Once he was well up the tree, two of the fellows slipped away and hooked up the fire hose and crawled back with it. Then they turned it on him.

That's when the noise began. I had forgotten to mention what

Bill had said to me, and Gene and I were both in bed. I jumped up and looked out of the little high-up window at the back of the tent and told Gene that the boy was up in the tree.

"This I must see," she said as she pushed her feet into her shoes, grabbed her coat off the rack, and dashed out of the tent. She had hardly gone a few feet before all the noise stopped except the hollering of the boy in the tree.

I learned later that Foster, Curry's son, had heard the noise, and with a bathrobe over his pajamas was seen coming down through the trees from his cabin on the knoll, close to where the Ridge Route starts.

Someone had given the alarm and the boys had dropped to the ground, which blacked them out. Just then Gene came from between the tents and stood wondering what was going on. One of the boys on the ground reached out and pulled her coat and said, "Duck, here comes Foster."

She turned and made a dash for our tent. Being the only upright figure, Foster sped in full pursuit.

She rushed into the tent and straight into bed and under the covers, shoes and all, and whispered, "Quick, get to bed." I did.

Almost immediately Foster hove into sight in the tent entrance and kept saying over and over, "It came in here, it came in here, I know it did." He even stepped inside and looked behind the trunk and looked down on us. We of course were sleeping beautifully, although ready to burst out laughing.

He went away and came back. We didn't dare move. At this point, there were several shrill screams from the direction of the road, and he dashed away to see what that was about.

When the boys went to the Village, they always used the side entrance by the oak tree. On this night, a group of them saw, as they turned in, several girls in the road in their nightgowns. They made a rush and surrounded them, and danced around them in a circle.

The girls had heard the yelling, as we had, and had sneaked out to investigate. At that time of night, the roads were usually deserted. So the girls hadn't bothered to put on their robes.

When Foster had come barging up to the circling boys and screaming girls, he didn't get any satisfying answers, and we could all hear every word he was yelling. He was going to start at tent one and investigate every tent, anyone not in their tent was going to be fired. Of course, everyone who heard immediately passed the word along.

Hal and George, who lived in tent one, had been in the Village, and returned just as the ruckus started and were told to get in bed and never mind undressing. So they did just that without knowing what had happened. When the covers were yanked off of them and they lay there fully clothed, they said, "Oh, we don't have enough covers, we always sleep this way." Other tents gave out various reasons for going to bed with their clothes on. I guess that Willie was about the only boy not in his bed. He was under Bill's bed, and Bill was snoring so loud and sleeping so hard Foster couldn't wake him. One of the boys who had been circling the girls was heard to say, "Girls are such sweet dear creatures, but why do they have to get us into so much trouble?"

Foster came back to the yelling Mr. X and ordered him out of the tree. "Shut that water off." For of course the fire hose had been thrown down and left running. Boy in tree, water all over, girls running around in their nighties, ropes and upside-down cots didn't make any sense, but he intended to trace it all to the bottom. Some guests in the morning said it had rained last night, some said that it hadn't, and so the crazy stunt kept getting worse.

So many innocent boys had been told to go to the office to get their paycheck that the boys decided they would all go. Soon the college boys had formed a serpentine line a block long, weaving in their college yells, that the whole camp, guests and help, was watching. Mr. Curry was standing on the platform by the office, waiting for the excitement to calm down. When they had lined up in front of him, he asked, "What do you want?"

"Nothing," they roared.

"What are you here for?"

"We've been fired."

"For what?"

"We don't know."

"What did you do?"

"Nothing."

Everyone got to laughing. Curry said, "There's hungry people to be fed, and work to be done, get to it."

A big yell went up, "What's the matter with Curry?" "Nothing, he's all right." The camp rang with their cheers as they disbanded to their different jobs.

Things were quiet for a few days, and they had to break loose again. This was a different fellow who worked in the office, a jolly good fellow who weighed around 300 pounds. He didn't have any offensive habit, but he had a routine that never varied. He took a walk at the same time every night around ten o'clock, always to the same place, for the same purpose, and he sat on the same seat. There happened to be a knothole in the fence guard in front of the cupola. That gave someone an idea, so the fire hose was hauled out again and put in position. It was another moonless night.

Sure enough, here he came, same opening, same seat. The signal was given, and the full rush of water hit the target.

The yell that went up was not the clerk's, it was the Stentor's.

Again the boys scattered, and water ran uncontrolled.

The fire hose was locked up. If there had been a fire the key would have had to be found.

There were many stunts that I heard about in a round-about

way and I am sure that there might have been many that I didn't hear of at all. It was natural that the college boys had their own groups and fun although many of them joined our groups at times, especially the Happy Isles picnics and big feeds.

One Saturday night Bill and I were sitting on a log in the meadow. It was strangely quiet. The Fire Fall was over and the granite background of Glacier Point was in the dark again. I ventured to inquire, "What's bothering you, Bill?"

"Yes, I am bothered. I'm leaving tonight to make a climb that has never been made before. I think that someone should know. I've decided that I will tell you. Don't you say a word unless I fail to come back. Failures are hard to live down."

I had never seen him so serious. I finally asked, "Where are you going?"

"I'm making a try for the south side of North Dome. I'll go up behind Washington Column to the base, just above the Arches. I'll try to get there around noon, while everyone is eating. I'd like to have you stand by the pool and wave to me. Then I'll make a try, straight up. Will you do that?"

"Aren't you going to take Pinkie or Willie along?"

"No, I don't want to risk any neck but my own. A few stupid moves of mine almost cost you your neck, and I haven't forgotten." He was quiet a few minutes, then he said very low, "You haven't answered me yet."

"Yes, I will be there watching," I assured him.

The next day I kept my word, and at noon I located him and waved. I tried to keep an eye on that moving speck all afternoon. I'd be making a bed and I'd leave it and dash out and look. Of course, in the Valley, when anyone starts looking, everyone wants to see, too. It was the longest afternoon I ever worked and I wanted to scream to everyone to look and see but I didn't.

With a good pair of glasses I would have been able to see the troubles he was in. I had to content myself by assuring myself that the little speck up on that granite slope was a little higher each time that I looked.

For a long time, he hadn't been able to move anywhere for the ledge had gone out to a point of nothingness and the handholds had gone with it. There was an object that saved him. Sometime in ages past a small seed had lodged in a broken piece of granite and started to grow, in spite of its disadvantages. It was more than his body-length away and his boots had been scraped shiny, which made them useless. Some way, just because he had to, he got his shoes off and let them roll down the side of the Dome. He had no assurance that the little limb hanging nearest to him would hold him, he would have to make a jump for it anyway, and his bare feet would have to save him now.

"Those few horrible moments, when practically hanging on nothing," he said, "I made the leap. The limb held, and I crawled up to the trunk and fairly collapsed behind it. I had lost my nerve. I would never be the first one to climb Mount Starr King. As a fearless climber, I was through. If I could make it back to camp I would have to finish out my working contract, and go home defeated in my own eyes.

"The rest of the climb was not too difficult, but my feet had been badly torn, and once on top I still had the long trip back via the Zig Zags.

"I found out in a way what you had gone through the night we had been lost. My feet would ache and ache until finally they would have no feeling, and I would realize that I was just pushing a stump out in front of me and falling after. Then all at once the pains would start again and I would realize I still had my feet."

Of course, he was telling me all this way after midnight. I had run to meet him staggering on the road from Happy Isles.

I had sat on the log seat outside our tent for hours, and in answer to Gene's frequent calls, told her I was soaking up moon-shine to take home with me. She finally had fallen asleep and ceased to call. I frequently would go out on the road to look for some movement on the road ahead.

My first words were "Where's your shoes?"

I'll never forget the heartbreak in his voice when he said, "I left far more up there than my shoes."

We went to the log seat in the meadow, where he told me what happened. He finished by saying, "If I had told the camp, I would have had to face their sympathy. No one knows but you."

I was able to help him to the washhouse, where he spent what was left of the night removing the scares of the climb.

When he appeared for work the next day barefooted, most people thought it just another one of Bill's funny ideas.

It was almost a week later when he had his accident. I think he was still under some kind of shock, for he had lost his caution. To make the extra money for the college courses he was planning on taking, he had assumed a double job. He was taking care of both the washers and the dryers. Besides these, he was in charge of the soap barrel. It had a steam pipe that went down inside it. When Bill turned to look at it, it was bubbling over. He ran his arm down through that boiling soap to shut off the valves. His burns were deep and painful. I wasn't there when it happened and he just would not talk about it. Naturally, everyone who saw his arm bandaged wanted to know what had happened. He just stayed in his tent. Everybody in camp was willing to suffer for him but there was nothing anyone could do.

Mother Curry came to me and asked me if I would get him out of camp during the day. "Get what you need from the kitchen. I think it will be easier for him."

We spent most of our time around Happy Isles, but if the tourists seemed to have gathered there we would go on further up the canyon, where I would cook our meals over a campfire, following his suggestions. The arm healed enough to take off the bandages and of course he could not work around hot steam for a while longer.

We were slowly ambling out of camp, headed for Mirror Lake. Bill was carrying the two-foot-handle frying pan and the coffee pot and the sack with the potatoes and onions, salt and pepper, with his good hand and arm, and I was carrying the steaks and bread and cold tomatoes. I don't know what was on his mind, but I was thinking how things had changed. He had stopped snapping at me and I had stopped snapping at him. He had progressed from hatred to disgust, from pity to kindness and understanding. I had progressed from bluffing and filed down some of the sharp edges of my tongue.

He was, after all, in his first year of college and I hadn't gone past the sixth grade. I had discovered that he liked to teach or rather tell me the way of things, and he had found out that I wanted to learn.

I remembered how nice Mother Curry had been when she came to me and asked me to take Bill out of camp through the day. "Keep him quiet if you can, feed him, and hope with us." After a little she had said so sweetly, "You two have climbed enough for this year, couldn't you sit quietly and talk for a change? Quietness and contentment can do much for healing, and the growing of new skin."

She was so right, for I had noticed the first trip out that he fumed and stomped around, and muttered about how stupid he had been and I could tell from the way he gritted his teeth that he was in awful pain. But now he just settled down and began talking to me about the Valley, and I would listen. Later he would hunt around for some fallen sticks or a small log and I'd peel the potatoes and slice the onions and set our pasteboard plates on a rock or on the tea towel with the silver, and he would sit close by and keep the jays and chipmunks out of the plates while I did the cooking. The heat of the fire only irritated the tender raw burned skin, so we ate quite away from the fire.

After we had eaten and I had sand-scoured the frying pan in the creek and left it on the rock to dry, and buried the scraps, I'd look over and see him drowned in thought. Then he would speak up and say, "Listen, the whole Valley is talking to us, a thousand eyes are watching us, and talking about us, and the trees are clapping their hands (leaves) because we look so funny. Our beautiful Mirror Lake is drying up and it is a pity. It is filling up with silt from the rock slides from Clouds Rest. The Valley is changing, day by day, the wind and the rain keep washing away the loose dust, and of course an earthquake is a fearsome thing when it breaks loose here and tears the rocks apart to make new changes. The Valley wasn't always beautiful as it is now, like when the glaciers were grinding their way down this canyon. In a few million years, it may be filled up and lose all its charm." Then he sighed and said, "Wish I had taken geology in high school."

I looked up, surprised, for any new word made me curious.

"Oh, I forgot," and he smiled. "That's the study about the rocks that make up this planet. Why, if I had studied geology, I could lie here and tell you the story that is written all over the face of Half Dome, or any rock for that matter. Muir could tell at a glance whether a glacier or a storm, or an earthquake, had scarred a rock, and when it happened. Remember those big boulders scattered over that smooth granite, in Little Yosemite, on the Merced Trail?"

I nodded.

"Well, that glacier may have carried those boulders clear from Canada, but there must have been a hot spell when they reached that little valley and the ice melted and left them there.

"I wish I had known Muir personally, but reading his books

is second best. All important men leave their thoughts in their books for others to read. That is why it is important to be careful what books you read. You can't live long enough to read all the great books, but you can do the best you can. Reading trash is like spending your time with a dirty, no-good drunken bum."

"How do you know whether a book is good or not?" I asked.

He looked up as he did when I asked something so simple, he couldn't believe his ears. Then he would remember and smile and answer slowly until I would understand.

"Didn't you have grammar, or English, or literature in school?"

"I had an English teacher and I guess she was getting around to those things in time, because we were reading something about some Greek people, and Fates and Furies and goddesses, when I first came to Palo Alto and was put in her class. She used to ask me to stand up and read for the class and said I was real good. I don't remember learning to read, I just seemed to have always read." And I laughed, "I even relieved the teacher in the first grade while she was busy with something else. That is the only thing I do know how to do if the words are not too big. But you haven't answered my question, how do you find out a good book from another until you have read it?"

He seemed not to have heard me and said, "I am puzzled about this teacher who at first thought you were so good, and yet didn't recommend or teach you from some of our classics."

"Your what? What are they?"

Well, he just sat up and stared. "There must be a story back of this mystery, and I'll answer your questions every one, if you will clear this up for me. Start at the beginning. You went into the first grade knowing how to read. What else did you learn the first day of school?"

I started to laugh, then said, "To be a crook."

Well, he sat bolt upright at that. I could see that he had forgotten his pain in the surprise. "How could you say such things?"

"I answered your question."

I was laughing so hard I could hardly tell him the rest of it, but he kept smiling and not knowing why.

"I didn't say the school taught me. You asked what else I learned the first day of school. O.K., I'll tell you, but promise not to tell." He promised.

"I think I must have gone to several first grades, for the first day in Los Angeles I got lost and had to be found and brought home. I remember a couple in New York. But this happened in San Francisco. Some boys were passing our house and Gene asked if they were going to the school. They nodded, so she said to me, 'You follow them.' She didn't say do what they did, that was my idea."

Bill was all attention so I continued, "I followed them and they stopped at a big gateway and picked up some shiny things that looked a little like pennies. I picked up some, and put them in my pocket. They stopped at a grocery store where there was a round glass bowl with a hole on top. I saw them put something in the top, and catch something in their hands under the bowl, so when I got there I did likewise. I put in the slug and caught the nuts with my hand when I noticed a very big man standing on the step above me. I came about up to his knees. He had on a big white apron.

"'What are you doing, little girl?' he said kindly.

"'Getting some peanuts,' I answered.

"'So I see,' he answered, 'and with what?'

"I held out a slug to him and showed him I had a pocket full.

"'Where did you get those things, little girl?' he asked.

"I pointed back up the street.

"'Enjoy the peanuts, little girl.'

"And I said, 'I will, thank you.'

"The next morning my slugs didn't fit the slot, they were too big."

Well, we had a good laugh, the first time Bill had really laughed since his injury. I thought that Mother Curry would be proud of me.

"What did you learn in first grade?" he asked.

I said, "I don't remember a thing, but at the end of the term I did get a pink card which was honorary. Papa was pleased and told me to always get pink cards. Well, I bounced around to fourteen schools in seven years. In the fifth I had been in a one-room school in the mountains and the teacher didn't know what to do with me. Every book she had I practically knew by heart, so she would give me a piece of paper and say, 'Write a story.'"

"Do you have any of them?" Bill asked.

"Just one, called 'My Life as a Pumpkin.' The title is still good. Don't you think?" So we had another burst of laughing.

"Well, let's get up to this school in Palo Alto, and this English teacher. What happened there?"

"Basketball."

Bill's eyes widened. "How could basketball hurt your English?"

"I knew enough not to go over in the boys' yard during school. But after school, I would go over on their side and play basketball with them, and I never missed a basket. I also used to go over to the high school and play basketball with the girls until they made me cheat. After I had gone with them to play Stanford University's girls' team and won the game for them, they told me I mustn't tell I was a grade school kid or it wouldn't count, it would disqualify them or something. I went back to play with the boys, they were more honest. I guess that was the reason she wanted to thrash me."

"You mean whip you?" And I nodded. "What did you do?"

"I was down on the boy's side playing with them, in my bloomers, the things were yards wide and made of serge. She called me from the window of the second floor, and I ran upstairs. She talked so fast, I didn't know what I had done. She reached for her beating stick and started up the next flight of stairs. I followed. Halfway up I had an idea, so I said, 'I hope you don't have anything to do this afternoon.'

"She asked, 'Why?'

"I said, 'I understand that you don't let anyone out of that room unless they cry, and I don't cry.'

"She turned around and passed me on the way down. I followed her into the room and she turned and said, 'It doesn't matter, Mrs. Amico said you were going to Hell anyway.'

"I said, 'I don't believe she said that about me, I'm going downstairs and ask her.' I loved that history teacher.

"The English teacher said, 'Don't you dare.'

"And I said, 'Well, then you are lying.'"

Bill's eyes opened wider. "You didn't!"

"From that day on, for almost a year, until Gene didn't let me go back last April, I sat in that teacher's room for the English period and she ignored me completely all except once."

"And that once?" Bill asked.

"Someone had put a small branch from a lemon tree on her desk and it had a lemon on it. I didn't know what it was. She held it up and looked at me and said, 'Laura, this is not funny.'"

"You poor kid," Bill said under his breath.

"Don't you call me poor," I said crossly. "I seldom have any money but I have never felt poor in my life,—I'd rather talk about the Valley anyway. Tell me more about this Muir guy."

"Don't you call Muir a guy, or I'll bat you one, I still got a good hand," he growled back at me.

Then we got to laughing again. On the way back to camp, he said, "What would you have done if I had biffed you one?"

I looked at him and grinned and said, "Nuttin'."

Mother Curry came up to me after supper and said, "You and Bill came into camp laughing, you're doing splendidly."

Another day we were sitting on an overhang, just a little bit up the Ledge Trail, after supper, watching the people in camp walking around. I saw a flower close by and said, "Bill, don't you know anything about flowers? You never mention them, only the primroses in the big meadow and the mariposa lilies on the Pohona Trail. Don't you like them?"

"Neither question is right. I do know them and care about them up to a point, but in Yosemite you can't mix birds and flowers with rock climbing. If you are up here to stroll around, why, watch the birds and the flowers, but if you are up here to climb, forget them. I came up here to practice for Mount Starr King, and of course that is over for now, so I didn't dare let myself be distracted by a posy on a cliff or a rare bird flying by."

"Do you know how many birds are up here?"

"I believe there are some 200 kinds of birds listed, not all of them native to the Valley, many stop in for a visit when they are migrating either north or south. They know a good thing when they see it." And he laughed.

"Do you know about the other things up here, too?"

"Oh, yes, let me think a minute, I had the list memorized at one time. Of course, that is for the entire park, not just the Valley. Yes, I remember, there are 1,300 kinds of flowers, 21 kinds of trees, 22 kinds of reptiles, and 65 kinds of animals. The bears roam all over the 1,189 square miles, 4 to 12 stay in the Valley." He smiled. "How's that?"

I clapped my hands.

"Speaking of bears, they are sure smart. They won't go into their dens no matter how cold or sleepy they are until there comes a snow with a wind. That's why you can't follow their tracks to find them.

"When you understand these so-called dumb animals, you get a real respect for them. Some people say that a rattler always warns you before he strikes. How dangerous to believe that, his tail rattles because he is nervous. The more nervous he is, the better it suits me, because many of them do strike without the so-called warning.

"A hunter usually goes into the woods loaded down with an accumulation of offensive odors about him, old leather, steel and iron, sweat, tobacco, gunpowder and often fear, which causes an awful smell. Then the hunter comes home and tells how nasty the animal was to handle. An animal has little chance against a bullet. An animal does not kill at a water hole, but man does. No wonder they want to get away from us.

"Why, I know a man who ran out of water in Death Valley, and was near dead, he managed to reach a water hole only to find several rattlers coiled around the edge of the water. Too far gone to care, he crawled between two of them, lay on his stomach, and drank, expecting to be struck a death blow any minute. Not one snake did more than look at him.

"Now you take this man Beebe,[12] and there's a man you should read. He used to go into the jungle in shorts and sandals, to get his creatures alive to study. He carried only a writing pad and pencil or pen. Sanderson[13] is another man for you to read. Both men loved the outdoors and what was in it. There are dozens or I should say hundreds of wonderful nature writers. Only most of them write so technically you wouldn't understand them. A librarian will help you select books if you ask her."

"I used to go to the library at Palo Alto and sit and read. But I never knew how to get a book to take home and I was afraid to ask."

12. William Beebe was an environmentalist who wrote primarily about jungles with a particular emphasis on bird evolution. He traveled around the globe from 1909 to 1914 studying pheasants, a trip that would result in his most famous book, *Jungle Peace*.

13. It is unclear what author by the name of "Sanderson" Pontynen was referring to here.

"I can't believe it," he said. "I practically lived at our library and would take home all the books I could carry, or the amount they would let me take out. Of course, my Dad bums property, but sometimes somebody will stand good for you."

"That lets me out both ways. Many people have loaned me their books and I am really careful of them. I wish I could take books home because I do want to learn."

"Gee, I wish you could go on with your education, especially in college. The professors would just love your inquiring mind. They get so fed up with the dumb bunnies that just sit and listen. I'll be your professor while I'm here." He laughed.

"For lesson one, how many flowers do you already know?" he asked.

I held up my hand to count them on my fingers. "I wouldn't know that many, I'm sure."

"You do the thinking, I'll keep the count."

So I said, "I know the poppies, I remember you called that pretty red-bell a columbine, and of course I shall never forget the snow plant. Then that stuff you called miner's lettuce, you made me eat, and the one you pulled up and used for soap, and called a soap plant, and that beautiful one that was orange with spots that you called a tiger lily, and of course I could never forget the azaleas. Then the ferns and wild roses, and of course the meadow primroses, and the mariposa lilies, I hope to see someday. I guess that is all."

"That's eleven, and about what the average person knows. Let me see how many I can recall and you keep count on me. I'm just an amateur though. The brodacia, golden, harvest, and common baby blue eyes that are around El Capitan in the early summer, pussy-paws, Queen Anne's lace, farewell to spring, Indian pink, larkspur, nightshade, yarrow, wild hollyhock, blue-eyed grass, buttercups, milkweed, monkey-flower, violets, goldenrod, fiddle neck, wallflower, shooting star." He started to laugh. "I'm supposed to know many more and here I've only, what?" I told him twenty-one. "I had better take some more botany."

There never was a teacher and pupil that had so much fun. Maybe another day we would count up the birds we could remember, or the animals, or the little life.

The arm was healing, and the days were getting closer to the time of his leaving. He wouldn't talk about it, and I really didn't realize it could happen until he waved from the bus and was gone. But we did have two nice long trips before he left. One was the Pohona Trail trip and we really did get in the Merced Lake trip also. It was Mother Curry's idea that Gene and a girl by the name of Wilson take us and go up to Sentinel Hotel for the night and come down the Pohona Trail in the early morning.

There were less restrictions on the Ledge Trail now that the water had dried up, so we went to Glacier Point by that route. We all started at the hotel, took pictures of each other on the overhanging rock, and watched the sun go down from Sentinel Dome. I climbed the Lone Pine to have a picture taken and realized too late that it was covered with the stickiest of pitches. Trees growing in rock cracks are a rare sight and this pine is probably the most famous of them all. The view of the High Sierras to the east with the afterglow was wonderful. The view of Half Dome looks even more scary than from the Valley. Camp Curry, straight down, looks so small, it's hard to believe but the Valley is not at its best from the top. To love something, you almost have to look up at it. It becomes just a hole with a river running through it, but we never ceased to thrill to the various other views that we took along the rim the next day. The first picture of the day was taken just as the sun was coming around the side of Half Dome. I was told that I would ruin the picture and it would be sun struck, but surprisingly it was clear and the sun looked like a pinpoint.

We then started out on the Pohona Trail, a beautiful trip of long stretches of meadows full of wildflowers and especially the mariposa lilies. Those little butterfly flowers with a touch of lavender, or a spot of yellow or soft russet on the petals. Dozens of shades of green, and we would swing along at an easy gait and go off sideways to take a picture on or from various points along the way. Gene had surprised us all by hiking in bloomers and I followed suit. I wondered what had happened to all this lady talk, but I was so happy to be free from the bunglesome skirts, I never questioned her decision in the least. My Dad maybe didn't see her ankle, but I or anyone else was seeing her entire leg and didn't dare tell her how pretty it was. Maybe my rebellion on Half Dome may have decided her and influenced her. I'll never know.

There was no particular hurry and we all enjoyed the trip. We took many pictures and there was one picture I hid from Gene. I looked so gaunt and I was afraid she might make me stop hiking and I did want to take the Merced Lake trip, and we took the trip soon after, leaving on a Saturday morning.

Mr. Curry was willing that we take the trip but insisted that another girl go along. Another girl was found willing to go but we had never hiked with her. She must have been a latecomer of the college crowd. I'll call her Lady X. She said she would go but she wouldn't walk it.

She got off on the wrong foot with us and stayed there. It nearly cost her her life and we were all responsible. We were all wearing out with too much hiking but we considered ourselves seasoned hikers, willing to take what came, whereas it could have been her only hike. Naturally, Bill, Pinkie, and I were all upset about her attitude, and I was telling Parsons how mad we were and he said, "No problem at all, take my horse. He knows the way right to my private fishing camp."

"Haven't you been living here? I've missed you with the crowd. Just thought you had found a better group."

"Never could find a better group," he answered. "But I have been going off on Saturday nights by myself to the lake, fishing all day, sleeping under the stars, enjoying the call of the wilderness, it could be the Indian in me. Anyhow I do have a camp up there and I always leave what food I have. The coffee pot is there with plenty of coffee, there's a frying pan hanging on a nail on the tree. You won't have to take a thing. Oh, maybe a loaf of bread. So have a good time."

So we left after supper that Saturday in early September with Lady X riding the horse. We all had a blanket tied to our back. We couldn't really set a pace of any kind and stay together, for she was forever making the horse trot. Pinkie was mad because he had to stay with her and go the long way to the top of Vernal Falls. Bill was mad because we were going to have to sit for an hour or two in the dark, there being no moon and wait for them. So the trip started out wrong in every way.

Then, too, the horse began to assert his view of the situation. He had made the trip many times and had his own shortcuts, and he took them. Being a white horse, we were able to follow, stumbling through brush and over rocks after that white rump until we were all furious. We couldn't try to keep him on the trail when we didn't know where it was ourselves. The girl was constantly hollering, "Stop him, stop him." She did have the boys help her off once, but it didn't do any good, she didn't know how to walk any better than ride, so she begged to be put back up on the horse again. So hour after hour we grumbled and stumbled along and were having a miserable time.

Finally, the horse stopped and would not go any further. We pulled and pushed, but to no avail. If he could have talked, he would have said plenty. I guess he was talking, only we didn't understand.

"Maybe we are there," Bill said, "Let's crawl around and see if we can find something civilized."

"Like what?" asked Pinkie.

"Oh, some campfire ashes."

"Maybe an Indian doesn't leave signs behind him."

"Parsons said he left a grub box hanging in a tree." I spoke up between chattering teeth.

"I just found it," Bill yelled. "From the bump on my head, it found me."

"What makes it so cold?" I asked.

"If we are where we are supposed to be, why, you are only a mile or so from a glacier," he answered.

"Everybody find some sticks so we can get a fire going," Pinkie said. "Hey, I think I have found the fireplace. I've just crawled into some ashes."

Bill followed the sound of his voice and the two of them chatted back and forth like a couple of magpies. "I got matches this time," Bill said.

"You better have matches," said Pinkie, adding, "Here's a pile of wood."

"Good old Parsons," answered Bill.

Soon a nice blazing fire was going, and Lady X consented to come down off the horse. She never said a word or offered to pick up a stick or join in any of our misery or our joy at finding anything.

I went over to the grub box that was hanging in a tree and opened it. It was empty. "Empty," I yelled and the boys came running.

"There's coffee in the can," said Bill, "but it is crawling." He took the can over to the firelight and called back, "Ants."

"The coffee pot is here, also the frying pan." I called to them.

"Good we got something," Bill said. "Good thing Pinkie brought his fishing pole and line, we won't starve. Besides, we have a loaf of bread." And he laughed, then said, "You can't blame this on me."

I had located a brush lean-to and flopped down under it, and came out as fast as I had gone under, followed by many squeaking and yelling forms running in all directions. The boys thought it real funny, and we were soon laughing. All except Lady X.

Mice, chipmunks, and squirrels. What of it? It was to be my bed, and I was tired enough to use it.

Seems that Lady X had lost her blanket. I told her she could crawl under mine.

"Not with all those wild creatures, I won't go to bed," she snapped.

"It's going to get pretty cold sitting under that tree when the fire is out," I answered.

I was soon sound asleep despite the fact that one little blanket wasn't much help against the cold. When I later felt her crawling in under the end of the blanket, I had the decency to feel sorry for her. It must have been after midnight.

When I opened my eyes again it was just breaking day. I crawled out and looked around. The white horse was munching grass about fifty feet away. About a block away in the other direction was a beautiful lake with cold, clear air, a birdcall somewhere, the smell of the pines and the glow of a rising sun. It was all so worthwhile, and way off through the trees was a herd of deer, unafraid and beautiful in their own world.

I looked over toward the fireplace, and Pinkie was sitting up. The sun was just touching his red hair, but I do believe his face was blue. He crawled out from under his blanket and picked up his fishing pole and motioned for me to follow.

I followed and he led the way to a small creek that ran into the lake. He threw a gunnysack to me and said, "Don't miss any, I'm starved."

If I thought it was cold before, I was dreaming. By the time I waded up that little creek behind him, catching fish he would throw to me, I really knew what cold was. Even the night I had been lost seemed mild in comparison.

When the sack was half full, Pinkie said he believed we had enough.

When we got back to camp, we found that Bill had built a warming fire, and a small one for cooking. He had found a level rock, and had the frying pan warming, and the coffeepot boiling, ants and all. With only one tin cup we had to take turns. But boy, that coffee was good.

Our Lady X was sitting wrapped up in all the blankets, with her back to a tree, eating a piece of bread.

The speed at which those boys went about cleaning those fish, all of them undersized, nevertheless they were fish and off came their heads and Bill took the cleaned fish and dropped them into that hot frying pan, and did they jump around.

We wild kids didn't wait for them to crust over. Bill found a piece of bark and flopped a half dozen onto it and said, "Eat," and I ate. He was dancing around with a couple between his teeth, singing and claiming he was an Indian snake dancer. Well, we ate until the sack was empty, but not our Lady X, she refused to eat live fish.

"They are not alive. Their heads are off and they have been gutted," Bill told her.

"They are too alive, look at them jump, trying to get out of the pan," she answered, nearly in tears. I think she was more scared of us than the fish.

The boys decided that little fish were very fine as a start, but out in the middle of the lake must be some whoppers. They had found a raft and assured me that for dinner we would have some nice properly crusted fish, broiled on a stick. Bill had scoured the frying pan with sand and hung it up clean and nice, also the coffeepot, as a proper woodsman should.

As they left to go on the raft, he turned to me and said, "You either duck that girl in the lake or we will when we get back, and you with her."

I did but of course, I had to convince her that I always swam in my khaki, and that the water was really warm, and that I loved it.

We lay in the sun after, and were nearly dry when the boys came back, without any fish.

While we were trying to decide whether to make a try for some more little fish and be late in starting back, or leaving right then, Willie appeared. He had decided to come along. He had left in the morning. He had walked the eighteen miles in good time.

"Got any food with you?" yelled Bill.

"No, why?"

Our stomachs decided the question, and we started back.

I said that I wanted to go on ahead and get a picture of a deer. I could sneak up on them whereas all of us would scare them. I left my blanket for the horse to bring back and Lady X to put around her. Riding even a little wet in the cold weather was still a dangerous thing to do whereas walking and keeping up the circulation, thus drying out little by little, was not too bad. Poor girl nearly died, I was told, for she got pneumonia and was rushed to the hospital. Willie had stayed with her and guided her horse back by the long trail. I'm sorry now but of course that doesn't help.

I had hurried on ahead, looking for a deer. I was coming along a fairly flat piece of the trail with some manzanita thickets on the right side, when out jumped a deer and planted herself spread eagle in front of me. It startled me, so I just stood there and looked at her for at least a minute. Finally, I said, "So you want your picture taken."

I proceeded to aim and get what I thought were two beautiful close-up views for she was only ten feet away. When the pictures were developed later they showed a head in one and a tail in the other. Was I teased, "No, no, no, you weren't scared," and they all laughed.

I had just completed the second picture when she glanced to her left. I looked also and there were her twins hopping along toward the edge of the meadow. As soon as they entered the protection of the trees, she bounded away. Who said that animals were dumb?

I went on joyfully and content, even with a near empty stomach. I had found a way of life and loved it.

I came to Sugar Loaf Dome. One that Bill had described to me, at one time, and he had said it had never been climbed, but he was going to try it sometime. It stood all by itself in an open plain. The oncoming glacier of a million or so years before had left it standing and gone about its business of strewing boulders all over the granite meadow.

Well, I stopped and looked at that Dome and decided that it didn't look so bad. I could see a really good ledge and some fine handholds. I started up and was doing fine until the ledge ran out and so did the handholds. I was perched up there feeling very guilty and wondering what to do when Bill and Pinkie showed up among the trees.

Bill was furious. "Dern kid, I've half a notion to leave you up there. But I'd have the whole camp to fight. Get those tennis shoes off and throw them down."

After I had done that, he said, "Now, press your feet as hard as you can against the surface, also your hands, and start inching your way down. If you lift them, you'll lose the suction and start rolling. You'll lose some skin off your seater, but that will serve you right for trying such a stunt on your own."

I made the bottom and he was right. I had left blood on another Dome in the Valley.

We dragged into camp sometime about midnight. As a trip, it

had been a failure and we had very little to say about it. It could have been a wonderful trip if taken earlier in the season, when it wasn't so cold and with a group that was agreeable, and with food to eat we might have seen some of the beauty. I had read once that the Indians of a southern desert did not see the mountains as beautiful. Maybe seeing beauty is an acquired habit, and needs a full stomach. At least I could understand the statement after that trip.

In a week, Bill would be leaving to go home. I never saw him again. He served in the war in the Signal Corps. Later he was in charge of some part of the construction of the Boulder Dam and was planning to go to Africa to build or work on some part of a dam.

Willie went on to be a teacher at the University of California at Berkley, Pinkie went back to Kentucky. I have never met anyone from camp after that summer of 1915 except Willie, I saw him once when Gene and I returned in 1917 for more adventures in my beloved Valley, Yosemite.

I looked around camp and realized how many others were leaving, and the hammers were starting again. The tents were coming down, the shelves in the laundry were filling up with mattresses and furniture. The dance space was getting smaller and smaller, and soon the college folks were all gone and there were Gene and I and a few other girls and the old bunch of "out-of-schoolers" left to pack up the camp for the long winter months and the cold. The days grew shorter, the sun lost its heat, the falls began to slow down and almost stop, at least the noises and music were gone and the Valley was quiet. It was Hell.

Green leaves turned to orange and brown and red and the meadows crackled as you walked over them. Autumn was there. Everything left in stages, Mr. Curry's voice would call out, "Farewell," and a great loneliness seemed to settle over all of us. No more pranks, no more spontaneous singing. The campfire was mostly deserted, the air was too nippy to sit still for long. Soon we would be leaving. I wondered where. Gene said we would not be going back to Palo Alto, but just where she hadn't said.

There were no big hikes, just local walks. But there was one I will never forget. Rummaging around in the trunk, I came upon my one party dress, and being bored, decided to put it on. I forgot that the group had decided to go to Vernal Falls to see the luna-bow and I was supposed to go along. Once dressed, there was no place to go but to the Campfire Circle, and I was there, sitting, feeling lost and alone and slumped down in the camp chair when the group came by.

"How come? Aren't you coming along?" someone said.

"She's not dressed for the trail, come on," said another.

"Bill's gone, maybe she is dolled up to catch another guy," said someone else.

They passed me by and turned up the road to Happy Isles. I never felt so deserted or unhappy. Of course, I could go back down to the tent and change, but by then they would be far ahead. I'd not be able to catch up with them. Well, I would go as I was, I might be a little cold, but that wasn't important.

I got up and went out on the road to discover that the dark seemed darker, the trees bigger and the falls having died down a little every noise seemed strange, but I kept on. Then the time seemed to drag. Surely, I should be getting there by now. The ground was covered with the fallen leaves of autumn, but even so I was sure that I heard steps. (I had forgotten that wild things don't make noise if they don't want to.) It must be a bear. Then I was sure it was a bear. I walked backward, I walked a step or two and would stop, I'd turn around again. When I went, it went; when I stopped, it stopped.

I must have taken the left-hand turn to Mirror Lake, I was going too far. I was close to being panicky when I saw the gleam of the light at the Happy Isles power house. I grabbed up my dress and fairly flew up the road and into the place.

I watched speechless as the attendant reached behind him for a rifle, and as he passed me he said, "Don't be scared any longer, little girl, I'll drive that bear on his way."

I turned to follow him, and heard the noise again, and in a flash, I realized what had happened. My three starched petticoats were rattling against each other. I marched outside and sat on the bench. I was so mad and ashamed I could have bawled.

"You don't have to sit out there, you can sit inside," he said to me. He tried to make conversation, but I maintained my stony silence. Even though I knew what it was that had scared me I still couldn't get up enough courage to go on up the Vernal Falls Trail, to where the others were, nor could I get up the courage to go back to camp.

Around ten o'clock I heard the group coming down the trail, all singing and having a good time. I could have been with them, hang the dress, I would never wear it again. As they came opposite me, I got up and joined them, walking by Gene.

"Oh, that's the fellow she dressed up for," some wisecracker sang out.

"He never even said good-bye to her, maybe they had a fight or something," spoke up another.

I was sure miserable, I was in bad no matter what, and I decided to keep still, which I did for many a year until I had grown up enough to laugh at my own silly doings.

Gene, of course, tried to quiz me, but I kept quiet, which made her more provoked than ever.

The following Sunday, the group went up to Happy Isles for a final good-bye picnic. I was up ahead with Hal and turned around just in time to see the power-house man come out and stop Gene.

They talked a few minutes, and later at the table she caught my eye and smiled, just a little too broadly to suit me. I was sure he had told her of my scare. She was a good scout, she never questioned me again about my lonely walk. I told her years later about my petticoat bear.

We folded blankets by the hundreds, and at the mangle folded sheets, to put away until the next year. The falls were quieting down and so were we. We walked and talked less, and every day there were farewells. We checked off the days that would mean it was our turn. We left in the latter part of September, and went to San Francisco, and by boat to San Pedro, and then on to Los Angeles. We returned in 1917 to the Valley land. I have added my account of it thinking that you might be interested in further accounts of what happened that year.

The Interlude

After Gene and I had left the Valley and until we returned in 1917, life continued to be a series of the unexpected, ridiculous, or near tragic. I'll tell about these twenty months briefly as they led up to and made our return possible.

After getting to Los Angeles, we stopped in to a candy store for a soda. I asked for a job and went to work the next morning for $7.00 a week and tips. Gene didn't get work for seven weeks. Then she went to work as a clerk for Hamburger's Department Store for $9.00 a week.

We had taken a front-room (one-room) apartment on Figaro Street, the kind where you sleep and eat and cook on a gas plate, do your laundry in the house bathtub, and hang things to dry over a line in a corner of your room, or leave the sheets draped over the chairs to dry while you go to work. Our new home had been a front room in its better days, and no doubt had faced a big lawn, but now the front window was just a few feet from the sidewalk.

The streetcar rattled by every fifteen minutes. The air was foul and the noise was a racket, and we had to go back to near-starvation meals, the kind that you leave the table hungry, two hotcakes and a cup of coffee for breakfast, nothing for lunch and a small piece of meat for supper, a boiled potato, a vegetable and you forget about there being such things as dessert.

The first night there I was awakened by such a lot of hollering, I hurried to the window and threw up the lower half, not knowing that the rope pulley was broken. About twenty men were outside, all talking a foreign language, and since we were

View of Yosemite Valley, 1915. Photo by Laura White, courtesy of Yosemite National Park Archives.

at war with Mexico and an invasion was expected, I was sure that was it. I turned from the window to answer Gene, who had wakened, and had asked what was the matter, and the window dropped down with such force that it cut three fingers to the bone, and I fainted. My invasion party turned out to be Mexican track workers and their supposed guns were only crowbars. The fingers healed slowly. I had gotten off to a bad start, I was an unknown casualty of that war on the home front.

The landlady's two daughters amused themselves by climbing up on boxes and peeking over the transom, so Gene went room hunting again. She got a room in the Grand Hotel (it had a gas plate) on the corner of 9th and Grand. A girl from Yosemite moved in with us until she could find a job. We were on the second floor with a brick wall three feet out one window, and a paved alley where the cats fought every night until I emptied a glass of water out of the window and the loud report it made when it struck, sounded like a shot. They scattered and never came back. Across the street was a "Dime-a-Dance" hall. None of us knew what that was and the two girls kept daring each other to go over and find out. It wasn't until a masquerade was advertised that they got up the nerve to go. The sign said "Ladies Free." Well, Gene went in one of her famous outfits called Equal Rights, half man and half woman, even her face was divided down the middle, a beautiful blonde with pink cheeks on the one side and an olive-skinned man with a mustache on the other half, with a fedora hat over his eye. On the upturned side the blonde hair was banked with flowers over the yellow curls. Louise went as a shepherd maid and I dressed as a gypsy.

We had no more than entered when we were grabbed and whisked onto the floor, and passed from partner to partner without so much as a "May I?" or anything else said. I fought free by the third ten-minute dance, and made for a stairway where I could climb and was able to locate Gene and Louise and motioned them to come on. We left. No more of that place. I weakened enough to go with them another time to a supposedly nice place. I danced one dance, when the owner got up on the platform and announced that there was a girl dancing who was not eighteen, and if she got on the floor again, he would remove her. That surprised me, because if dancing was O.K. what difference did it make? If it was bad, why dance? I sat the rest of the evening on the sidelines, and that ended any dancing for me in Los Angeles. I stayed home and either did embroidery or crocheting. Later, I joined the YWCA and had fun there.

The next night or two after the masquerade I was asleep on the couch while Gene and Louise were getting dinner when the fire alarm went off. They each grabbed a hand and dragged me into the hall. The hall was so full of black smoke you couldn't see at all. Half asleep I broke loose. They grabbed for me and got each other and got out of the building before they discovered their mistake. I was told later that Gene had sure raised a ruckus. As for me, I had gotten back into the room, noticed the thick smoke coming in over the transom, shut it, and went back to finish my nap. The firemen had come looking for me but they searched only the halls. Half the hotel started the fire and burned down the other half.

Hours later I was awakened again and someone was pounding me and screaming. Louise stopped her and quieted her down. Poor Gene had again worried herself sick over me only to find me O.K.

Gene went out again to hunt for a room, this one was on Francisco Street. A front-room apartment with a two-burner gas plate in a closet on an apple box. We lived there until we went back to Yosemite in 1917.

The job I was so proud of getting turned out to be terrible, it seemed to me, because I had never worked around the kind of people that worked there. They even had a sign up that said "Do not talk dirty where the customers can hear you." To them an acceptance of filth was a sign of being adult. To make matters worse, I had the midnight shift, which meant I had to go down onto Main Street to catch a car to go home. I was scared of the drunks who would surround me and try and pull me down the street. I would hang on to the telegraph pole and never say a word, and they would finally go on saying I was no fun. I used to wonder why people said the mountains were wild and danger-ous.

When Gene got her job, I asked her to get a job for me at the same store. She was fortunate and I was to go to work for $4.00 a week as a messenger, but I was under sixteen and I had to get a permit from the school department.

Gene had to make the trip with me on her lunchtime and was real put out about it. When we got there and went into the office there was a young woman leaning on the counter talking to the clerk and she was heavily made up. We waited and waited and finally Gene said, "What do I have to do to get attention around here? Put some paint on my face?"

The woman left in a huff, and the clerk threatened to put Gene in jail for making me work, and put me in a reform school for working. Gene got huffy and slammed out of the office.

I stood there and he yelled at me, "What do you want?"

I was growing up fast. I said calmly, "What I came for."

He hit the ceiling again.

I said, "Now, please listen, I just quit a job where I have been working for over seven weeks for $7.00 a week and tips and I am taking a job for $4.00 a week to get away from it. Does that make sense? I've worked since I was ten and for wages for over two years. What would you gain by locking me up?"

He looked at me as if for the first time and said, "Go tell that woman to come in here and sign the paper, but keep her mouth shut and I'll give you the permit." And he did.

There was a condition to it, I had to go to night school. They were so concerned for me I could have laughed. But I had to obey them. So I got up at six, dressed and got breakfast and did up the dishes, while Gene made the bed and tidied up the room, we then walked fourteen blocks to work and got there by 8:30.

As a messenger, I was running all the time and because there was a war on, they took one half hour of our lunchtime to go up on the roof and drill. Why, I never knew. I guess I needed the exercise.

We each had a dime for lunch, only I never used mine because that was the only way I had of getting any money. And being a messenger, I was supposed to join the YWCA on 3rd and Hill and go once a week. After some more walking, I was to buy my dinner, which took twenty-five cents out of my sixty cents, and walk home afterward alone.

I had to run all morning and afternoon, and except for that one night, walk home, get supper, wash the dishes, while Gene washed clothes in the tub or ironed, then walk ten blocks to the night school, stay until nine o'clock, walk back and go to bed. I was sure that if I lasted until my birthday, I would indeed be lucky.

Later, because I was fast on my feet, the store manager thought I had a super-brain, so he made me a special messenger, to work out of the office and run down to the bosses. Then I was advanced to be a wrapper, and then to the stock room, and then to the comptometer room and finally my name was suggested to a lady who gave me a scholarship with the promise of an office job at the end of nine months (at the store for $125.00 a month).

It meant that I had to walk ten more blocks a day, and we

had to live on Gene's wages. That meant after the rent was paid ($10.00), $5.00 for food and all supplies a week, there was $6.00 left for clothes and a few other items we might need.

No one had asked me what I knew, and I knew very little. Bill had convinced me that I needed more schooling. It never dawned on me that they would refuse to teach me, but they did.

I sat in the room for two weeks and was never asked a question. It was the same old freeze-out again, then one afternoon I stayed in after the others left and faced the professor.

"When are you going to teach me something?" I asked.

"I'm not," he said. "I'll bet you haven't even finished grade school."

I shook my head. Then I got mad and said to him, "If you think I am going to go back to that store and admit that I am stupid, you're mistaken. I am going to come down here every day and sit there and stare at you, all day."

"I'll bet you would." And he started to laugh. He turned out to be one of the best friends I ever had. He opened the doors to a world more bright. He loaned me his library card and sent me to get books under his direction. The first book I was able to take home and read was *Innocents Abroad* by Mark Twain. And he explained how writers used different names to write under, and that the man's real name was Samuel Clemens.

He used to give me a dime, paper, and pencil and send me out to take a car ride to the end of the line and I was told to write down what I saw, and thought. I finally was able to type slowly and I mastered the shorthand if it was given slowly. He would give me work, study, letters to copy, spelling to work on, typing to practice, then send me out to watch an office and answer the telephone for maybe a quarter. Then one day he found me a job for fifty cents a day and it was regular. I was to open the office in the morning and answer the phone and close the office at five if the boss wasn't there. To be paid each day, he was told I had to use it to buy supper with.

The boss came in one day and found me typing, and he said, "I suppose you know how to write letters."

"If they are not given to me too fast," I answered.

He agreed to pay me twenty-five cents for each letter I wrote for him, and all went well until he complained that I didn't wear silk waists like the other girls in the offices. If my clothes were on his mind I felt that the job was on the way out.

One Saturday morning I asked Gene to get me a package of Snow White to clean my tennis shoes, because I had been invited to Glendale for Sunday, to visit one of the messenger girls.

Gene went to the shoe department and bought the box with her employee's discount, and asked the floorwalker to sign the package so she wouldn't have to stand in line at the window to get it. She explained that I had to get a certain train. He refused.

Gene said, "Well, never mind then, I'll pick up a bottle of it at a drug store on my way home."

He reported her and said she was disloyal to the store and they laid her off.

I knew that my job was shaky and I was so homesick for fresh air and running streams of pure water. I would sit and dream of Yosemite, all its beauty I was missing, and I was miserable.

Then one day the boss asked me to write a letter to the owner of the Yosemite Falls Camp in Yosemite. I jumped at the chance.

"Do you know him well enough to ask him a favor?" I asked.

He said he did and in a few days Gene and I were headed back to Yosemite, supposedly to a job in the backcountry in charge of one of the camps. Gene was to go as cook and I was to take care of the dining room. We planned to switch jobs later as she hated to cook, and I thought I knew how.

All of my stay in Los Angeles hadn't been awful. The YWCA ar-ranged for a two-week camp for me the first summer, and I got to climb Mount Baldy. The second summer on Gene's vacation we had been invited to go with friends of hers to their cabin in Pacoima Canyon for two weeks. That trip decided me as to my life work, I would be a ranger. It also caused more grief for Gene. Gene's friend had brought a neighbor boy, about twelve, to be company for me. It was his first trip to the woods and he was uneasy and scared. I felt years older but tried to be patient as Bill had been with me.

The cabin was one room about fifteen feet square with a rock fireplace outside for cooking. The walls were wood up to about four feet, the rest was screen to the roof. Gene and I slept outside on a set of springs with a mattress wedged in between a couple of trees. We used to lie there and enjoy the moonlight and especially the early mornings when we might see a deer or a fox and especially the little skunks that stand on their heads with their tails drooped over them like an umbrella. One morning we woke up and saw two rows of mountain lion tracks close up to the bed. We certainly had been sniffed at during the night; that decided us, we went inside. I slept with our hostess and Gene made her bed on the floor. The boy was sleeping on a wooden seat, then the storm hit.

The canyon is only a half mile to a mile wide in places and the thunderclaps sounded over and over each time and the lightning was terrible. The water rushed into the cabin, and over Gene, and before morning we were all wet. The next morning every bush was hung with bedding. We were wondering how an old man up canyon fared in the storm and decided to walk up there and find out. We were talking to him when a ranger came by loaded with firefighting equipment.

"Got a fire up ahead, lightning did it. When the others come let them know I've come through," he said as he passed us.

When he had disappeared around the bend in the trail the boy said, "Let's follow."

We took off on a run but only from bend to bend, feeling

that he wouldn't want to be followed. Finally, we lost him and were standing in the trail wondering where he had gone when he called to us from the upper trail, there being a switchback on ahead.

"What do you want?"

"I want to see the fire," the boy said.

"Well, come on," the ranger answered. The boy took off on a run up the main trail and doubled back up to the upper trail till he caught up with the ranger.

I thought it very foolish to go running on an uphill climb so I followed in a more leisurely way. I went about three or four miles before I saw smoke overhead, above and behind the embankment, and I had to go on to a point to the right before I could look back and see where the fire was. The entire side of the mountain was ablaze.

The ranger was yelling at the boy to look out for the falling rocks that were hot because the brush or needles holding them had been burned away and they would roll downhill, starting a new blaze.

I yelled, "Yoo-hoo" and got a good cussing. "Go home, you dern kid."

I yelled back, "Do you need any help?"

"I sure do" was the answer.

"Who shall I get?"

"Anybody."

So I took off on a run back down the trail and it was now full of tracks of animals run out by the blaze and the valley to the left was noisy with the calls of the wild animals. I could still see the trail, which was about three feet wide. It was real dark when I reached the trail above the switchback, and I decided to slide down to the trail below to save time. I started a fair-size slide and landed at the bottom with all of it around me.

Two rangers had been standing at the branching trail not

knowing which way to go and heard the noise I made. They came running back down the trail and helped get me out.

"Where did you come from?"

"The fire," I answered through a mouthful of dirt, and they gave me a drink out of their canteen. I then told them what was happening up there and one of the rangers gave his pack to the other, and taking his shovel, started out at a fast gait.

I thought I had done my part and was through but the ranger said, "Oh, no, you don't. You're going with me." So up the trail I went again. When we reached the inside curve of the trail, with the smoke and crackling noises above us, he said, "I hope you are not afraid, because I can't go back with you."

What good would it do to be afraid? I thought. One place was as bad as the other.

"Did you ever cook over a campfire?" he asked.

"Yes."

"Fine." And he dropped his two packs and proceeded to chop up some wood and limbs he found near. He built one fire for light and warmth and piled up some small pieces for the cooking fire, and even piled up some rocks so that the frying pan and the coffeepot would sit on them. I was to light the small fire when he shot off his pistol. He opened the big can of beans and set it in the frying pan for me to empty when he was ready, and put water in the coffeepot. Then he took off his coat and told me to put it on and, taking his shovel, he climbed the bank and was gone.

The animal noises on the one side and the yelling above were bad for a while and I went out on the point so I could look back and see what was happening. I stayed out there until I got pretty cold, and went back to put on more wood for the big fire. Then I curled up in the corner of the curve and went to sleep, although I hadn't planned to.

The shot awakened me and I soon remembered where I was and why, and I carried a burning stick from the big fire and lit the smaller pile, dumped the beans into the skillet, put the coffee on and sat down to wait. It was then that I noticed a light way down the trail and decided to build up another fire further out so I could see who was coming before they got too close to me. I watched that light come closer and closer till it rounded the bend in the trail, there was Gene.

"There she is," she yelled. She couldn't come by the fire and she was mad. She had an old man with her, about seventy years old, and he didn't seem at all happy being there. "You come with me this instant," she called to me.

"I can't," I said. "I'm working for the government." I took the axe and dragged the partly burned log back to the other fire, along with the brush, and then Gene and the man came on down the trail.

About ten minutes later the pebbles and dirt began to roll from the bank above us and the ranger and the boy slid into camp supporting the first ranger between them. He had been hit in the hip by a hot boulder and was in quite a bit of pain. The ranger gave him a tin cup of hot coffee and then turned to the old man and said, "Good, I am glad you are here. Go on up there and take this man's place."

"I don't think I can," the stranger said.

"You get up there and try," snapped the ranger and the man started up the side of the embankment.

The ranger then squatted down by the fire and wrote on a paper and handed it to me. "Do you know Lake, at the entrance of the canyon?"

I said I did.

"After you two girls get this man to his home you can give this note to Lake and wait until he loads up a knapsack with food, and bring it back up here in the morning." And he added, "Don't let that boy come back, he's a nuisance."

Gene and I got the injured man leaning on our shoulders and

started down the trail with a very tired boy following. Gene held the lantern, but it was very slow going and agony for the ranger.

Seems like the boy had tried to help but did more harm than good, and when ordered to get out and go home, couldn't find his way back to the trail. He was then ordered to get out of the way, which he did until the other ranger came. When the third ranger arrived and was ready to come down and eat, he had ordered the boy to come try and help get the injured ranger down the incline.

It was dawn before we got the injured man to his cabin and then Gene and the boy dropped off at our cabin to reassure the woman that we were all right. Gene said she would get breakfast and for me to stop and get something to eat before starting back up the trail again. I would have covered at least twenty-six miles since I had eaten and it would be maybe sixteen miles before I would eat again.

When I returned and was resting, I found out what had happened the night before. When we hadn't returned, Gene started out to find someone to go with her to hunt for me, about a mile down canyon she found the old man in a cabin and said he had to go with her. He refused at first, but he didn't know Gene. When they got to the switchback and found the slide and my tennis shoes mixed up with the footprints of the two rangers Gene was really worried. However, my tracks were easy to follow.

She finally reconciled herself that I was working under orders and said no more.

I carried food up that trail three days and in due time received a check for $3.50. I was so thrilled and proud of those wages. I had proved to myself that I could be of service and that I didn't grumble under orders. I bought me a carbide light for future trail use.

Gene would shake her head and say, "What next?" Worse was

to come. Indeed, I never knew why it seemed that everything I did or planned got out of hand, and life was never dull.

That night decided me, I was going to be a ranger. They said I had to wait until I was of age. I studied and read all I could find that I thought would help, but when I became of age and wrote to headquarters, they wrote back that they didn't hire women.

Yosemite
1917

As I had said before, my fifty cents went for buying our dinner. I had found a butcher that gave me a real big piece of meat for a dime, sometimes a steak or two chops, a vegetable stand that gave me lots of vegetables for a quarter, and a bakery that sold a big loaf of bread for a nickel. The other dime went for beans or coffee, eggs, or for something else.

When I told these merchants that I was leaving they seemed so sorry and said I would need a lunch for the train. The butcher gave me a big order of cold cuts, and the vegetable man gave me fruit, and the bakery gave me bread and cookies.

Gene and I tried to eat it all and arrived in Yosemite very, very sick. One look at us and the boss said, "Neither of you are fit to work. Go over to the barracks and find a couple of cots that are not made up and I'll have some bedding sent over. And as for the job, I wouldn't send you two girls back in the high country, it's too dangerous. I'll find you something else to do, I'll send for you in a few days. You eat in the building back of the kitchen."

So Gene and I, with our queasy stomachs, found our way to the barracks, jobless, penniless, but happy that we were back in Yosemite.

Where we were to sleep had actually been the barracks used by the soldiers when the military were helping to run the Valley. Canvas had been run the length of it about two feet apart, making an aisle, then it was divided by canvas every ten feet, making rooms. It was used for the girls only.

Two days later we were told to report to the laundry. We were both experienced and were both put on the mangle. The work was similar to Camp Curry, but that was all. The fun and friendliness weren't there. There were don'ts all over the place. Don't go here and don't go there. The guests stayed by themselves, and so did the other help. Outside of two or three people I never saw any other workers besides in the laundry. It was terribly depressing. Worst of all was the shock of the food, and the way it was served. There was a long table with benches. The oilcloth had been scrubbed clean of design. A group of men would come in and crowd onto the benches and were there to eat and not to talk.

Big platters were set at the end of the table, and as they passed you, you either took what you wanted or went without. The men neither cared to know you or have you know them, they wolfed down the food and got up and left. I supposed that they worked somewhere about the camp, but never saw them anywhere. I ate by a girl who also worked in the laundry and she wouldn't touch the meat, said it smelt, and would make you sick. She ate only the vegetables and drank milk and stayed well. It took about three sick spells before I followed her system and stayed well, too.

Of course, if I hadn't been sick I probably wouldn't have met Harry. I was sitting out back of the building holding my stomach when he came by with a tray. He worked as a bus boy in the adjoining lodge of tents and used to carry breakfast to some of the guests. The next day was a Sunday.

"You're new here, and sick already, too bad."

I nodded.

"Have Ollio stay in with you tomorrow morning and I'll bring you both a tray from the guest's supply." I did as he suggested, and what a wonderful breakfast she and I had. Everything tasted wonderful.

Later when he invited us to join a group that had a picnic by the falls on Sunday afternoon, we went and took Gene and in that way we got in with a nice bunch of kids that were just as disgusted as we were. I would never have believed that I would be unhappy in Yosemite, but I found out that you can be miserable anywhere. Being asked to join with this group made the future look better. Of course, they had to pool their money and buy the picnic, because there was no going to the kitchen and getting anything, so their picnics were simple sandwiches and coffee, but they were sociable and I was grateful. There being no tips, I had no money while I was up there that year.

Just before you get to the lower falls (Yosemite), on the left side of the path that led in from the road, there was a huge cave, probably twenty feet square, and the roof slanted up and outward. It was a safe place to build a small fire and sit and talk, and that was where this little group had its little picnics. They weren't very interested in hiking or getting up on a mountain or any of the trails or peaks although I did talk a few of them into making a try for Clouds Rest. That nearly cost me my life. Harry arranged for a horseback ride that proved a near disaster, another time a swimming trip went to the bad also. The job proved to be dangerous, too, in fact, everything seemed to go wrong in the three months we were there. However, if we hadn't been there we wouldn't have heard of a job that took us back and forth across the United States several times in the years that followed.

The second Sunday we met with the group, they told us of a little backwater cove away from the main current of the river where they had been swimming and asked us to go with them. One of the boys had a rowboat hidden in the underbrush and they filled the boat once with Olive and me and rowed across to a sand pit to sun and dry out after a swim. I was just learning to float and had stayed in the water a little longer and was by myself floating close to the bank, so I thought, when the current caught me and whisked me into the center. As I was struggling, I remember seeing Gene on the opposite bank, pointing my way and screaming. Just then I disappeared around the curve, headed for the main part of the river. The thought came to me, that if I would stop fighting the water I'd be all right. I floated easily but too fast to suit me and I began to paddle toward the left bank. When I was going under a limb I reached up and grabbed it. I pulled myself over to the side, climbed out none the worse except for a moment of terror, and walked back toward the cove.

Gene of course was furious and said no more swimming in the river. I disobeyed her on the following Sunday, when I was out alone walking up by the Arches. I should say that I meant to sneak a swim with a group that was having fun in a shallow place by the bridge. I was leaning on the bridge railing watching them when a woman called to me, "Want to come in? I've got an extra suit here." And she pointed to the bank, where a suit was lying.

I went down the bank and picked up the suit and said, "Where do I change?"

She pointed to a tent about fifty feet away, so I went up and changed and left my clothes lying across the bed, and returned to the river's edge.

"I left my clothes in your tent," I said.

"That's not my tent," she replied.

"Whose tent is it?" I asked, alarmed.

"I don't know," and she laughed. I fell all over myself getting back up that bank, and the most agonizing next ten minutes of my life getting back into my clothes. I looked around the tent and there wasn't anything feminine, anywhere. Suppose those men would come back and find me dressing. A thousand "ifs" and "supposes" went through my mind, but I made it out of there safely. Served me right for trying to put one over on Gene.

Since I couldn't go near the water because of orders, Harry suggested getting horses and going for a ride. I told him I could sit on a horse standing still but wasn't sure what I'd do if it started moving, so the barn boy gave me a real old, slow nag that wouldn't jolt a baby. Harry had a fine black mare that could have been a one-time racehorse.

We went toward Bridal Veil Falls and incidentally got one of the finest pictures of the falls I have ever seen, but it so happened that Harry was holding the horse and had his back to the camera, so I never got a picture of him. He had a pleasant, happy face and laughed a lot. When he enlisted to go to France a few weeks later I was sorry I hadn't take a picture of him that day.

We started back to the Valley when he suggested that we switch horses. He said I was doing fine. We switched and I must have done "finer" for he suggested that we do a little racing, just back and forth on the road for a mile or two. That went fine, until the horse decided she had had enough and there was some barley at the barn. I had only one thing to do and that was hang on. We streaked past a couple of cars, went through the main center of resting tourists, passed the barracks, and out of the corner of my eye I caught a glimpse of Gene throwing her arms in the air, as if to say, "She's at it again." I don't know who alerted the rangers, but all at once there was a ranger on each side of me, and they crowded my horse into a place where two buildings came together. When their horses rammed against mine I was sure both of my legs were broken. My horse reared up snorting and, in the excitement, I was lifted off. When I found out that I could still stand, I got hysterical (glad in reverse). The ranger started to shake me. "This is not funny, Miss!" he repeated several times. I went over and sat under a tree until Harry came walking in on dear old Grandma.

When Gene found me, it was a promise, "No more horseback riding."

Well, I couldn't swim, I could not go on a horse, and nobody wanted to hike. I'd settle down to a quiet Sunday, stay at camp, so I gathered colored grasses from the marshy places close to the river, picked up some pieces of bark, took possession of a vacated spot in the barracks and borrowed a pocket knife, and decided to amuse myself for the day. In gouging out the bark for some purpose, the knife slipped and cut deep between my thumb and first finger on my left hand. So that was the end of that project. With unhealed sunburns on my shoulders that bled every time I lifted my arms at the mangle, and two badly bruised hips, and a crippled left hand, I figured I would spend the next Sunday doing my ironing, as my right hand was still in good condition.

The boss and several others were in the laundry when it happened. I had finished and reached up with my right hand to throw the switch, when the electricity went through me, some way my finger had gotten between the switch and the contact. The pain was awful for a second. When I came to, I was on the floor with my head in the boss's lap.

The next Sunday Harry and I went for a walk, just around camp, and stayed awhile in the open-air resting circle in front of camp. We got up to cross the road, surely nothing could happen, but it did.

We stopped to let a farm wagon go by. The boy driving it we knew by sight because he delivered the milk to all the camps both morning and evening. We knew that somewhere in the direction of El Capitan was a dairy. We noticed the boy was doubled up in the seat, and ran out to the wagon. The horses stopped, and we climbed up beside him. He was moaning something awful. He kept saying a name and mentioned Modesto. "Call him, please," he said and then he passed out. Harry took the reins while I supported the boy, and we made our way to the hospital. A doctor and a nurse soon relieved us of our patient. The boy's appendix had burst or was about to. The doctor said, "You kids better deliver the milk, the hotels will be looking for it."

So we would drive up to a kitchen door and tell our story and say, "How much do you take?"

At one place someone said to us, "You better let his boss know about this. He has a ranch or dairy near Modesto." After we had delivered all the milk and gathered up the empty cans from the morning delivery, we went to the telephone office, and with the help of the man there, located the boss and told him what had happened.

"Be sure and get the horses back to the barn and see that the cows are milked in the morning about five o'clock. I can't get up there before tomorrow about two, but I'll bring a new boy along. Just take care till then." And he hung up.

Harry and I just looked at each other and started to laugh. Get the horses back to what barn and where? Get the cows milked how and by whom? Well, we couldn't do all that and stand there laughing, so we started out asking everyone we met, "Can you milk?" "Can you get up at five in the morning? Do you know where the barn is?" All we got was "No, no, no" from every man we asked. So we started in on the women. Bless their hearts. We were lucky and found a woman who had been raised on a farm. "No cow is going to suffer if I can help it. You find the barn and let me know. I'll be there." We found six girls who would milk the cows, if we could find them. So we started out to find the barn. Of course, we never thought to find a lantern first, and the horses being smarter than we were just started out and we let them go home. When they stopped, we got out and found their noses up against a gate. We opened the gate and they went in.

"Did you ever unharness a horse?" I asked Harry.

"No, but I can try."

We finally loosened up every buckle we could find and got the horses out of the shafts and said, "See you in the morning." And shut the gate behind us.

Harry said, "Now the question is, are we as smart as they are? Can we find our way back to our barns?" What a night.

Six girls were up and into borrowed overalls by four in the morning, following me to the west. These girls knew something, for they found the cows and sat on the stools except one who was told, after the cow had kicked her off the stool, that the moo moo was dry. One of them found a calf and turned it over to me. "Nothing to it, just put some milk in a bucket and put your hand down into the bucket and let the calf suck your fingers, it won't know the difference."

"But will I get my fingers back?" I asked. I was told to run if the bull looked at me, I sure did. I had on a red ribbon. Those ex–farm girls were really heroes and finally they harnessed the horses and Gene drove, and we started out to deliver the milk.

"What are you going to get into next?" she asked me.

The dairy man arrived as promised and left two five-pound boxes of chocolates for the girls. Harry and I never saw a piece of it.

I decided that the next day off I would go to the picnic, it ought to be safe and sensible, but it wasn't. It was the day after the Fourth of July. Harry and I had been left behind to put out the fire. It was just getting dark, and we were carrying the cans of water from the creek when I noticed a spiral of smoke coming from the ground between the trees about fifty feet away.

I said to Harry, "Go back to camp and tell the ranger to send someone down here with a shovel and a bucket. I'll wait till they come. It might be too dark soon and they may not be able to find the smoke." So he went running off through the trees. I finished putting out the fire in the cave, and went to stand in the path and wait.

In about fifteen minutes, I saw a ranger racing his horse

down the little road, and he dashed up and yelled, "Where's the fire?"

"Over there." I pointed to the spiral of smoke.

He seemed to think it very funny for he threw his head back and roared with laughter.

Well, I didn't and I told him a few things, including how stupid he was and started back to camp. I had gone only a little way when I heard plenty of noise and hollering and there came the firefighting equipment. Rangers and volunteers were hanging on the sides and rear.

Being laughed at once was enough, so I took off on a run through the trees. I heard the voices of the law yelling, "Stop!" But I didn't.

I found Harry on the rangers' steps with a big grin on his face.

"What's the big idea?" I demanded.

"Well, it was this way. I didn't want you waiting down there too long. I got up here out of breath and tired, so I told them that it was a big fire and you were in the middle of it. You should have seen them go into action. They didn't even notice that I didn't go along."

"You don't yell, 'Wolf, wolf,' about fires," I snapped at him and walked away.

I went over to the outside sitting place, to hide out amongst the tourists. I was in an ugly mood and didn't want to talk to anyone. I got to thinking of that fire in Pacoima Canyon and the hurt ranger. When I looked up and saw the person of the law heading my way, I jumped up to beat it when again I was yelled at to "STOP." This time I did.

When he got up to me I snapped at him, "I guess you want to laugh at me, too."

"No," he said in a quiet, controlled voice. "I came to thank you. If it hadn't been for you, I might have had to order all these people out of the Valley tonight."

"Well, just the same, someone else can find your fires for you."

"Young lady," and his control was slipping, "if I ever find out that you saw a fire and didn't report it, I'll arrest you."

"Better teach your rangers some sense then," I replied heatedly.

"I'll take care of my rangers, Miss. That fellow is new, and probably had an idea of rescuing you. He has never seen a forest fire or seen his buddies burned up, but he will someday, and he will remember you then." He grinned, "After all, considering the yarn your friend told us."

"No friend of mine," I broke in.

"So I understand. He is in the doghouse for this, so he said. He told me where you were. You see, you were going so fast this evening I had only a rear view—I had to find out who you were so I could thank you."

My temper had cooled, so I grinned and said, "O.K., I'll find your fires for you. I always wanted to be a ranger, but this is a man's world. You want our help, but you shut us out."

"You qualify, and I'll recommend you." Then he told me how they had found a buried rocket that had exploded underground and it was really dangerous conditions. The men had dug down about two feet to get to the blaze. A squirrel runway had probably given it the air that had kept it going. All it needed was more air and the Valley would have been a blazing inferno by now.

"Thank you again," and he tipped his hat and was gone.

I thought I saw Harry peeking around the tree at me, but I had had enough talk for the night, besides, all those people were staring at me as though I had stolen the hotel silver, so I went on to the barracks.

A few evenings later Harry and I were returning from a dance at Camp Curry, and I saw where a discarded cigarette had started a fire in the meadow. Harry wanted to stomp it out, but I said I had to make my word good with the ranger, so we ran to the ranger station, we busted in, clicked our heels, saluted, and said together, "Fire in the meadow, sir."

Bells started ringing, but the ranger wiped the grin off my face by saying, "You are still on probation for running away from the law, TWICE, now stop your clowning." Two weeks later one of his rangers nearly shot me. Yes, I have either been a help or a hindrance to rangers. But how does a girl qualify?

The next Sunday I decided to get out of camp. I asked one of the girls to go on a hike. She had never hiked or been on any of the peaks and was so thrilled after coming back, she talked four others into going the next Sunday to Clouds Rest.

I said, "Surely we are entitled to some food whether we eat it here or on the trail. Let's raid the ice-box." In the dark we located a pie, some coffee, a couple of loaves of bread, some bacon, and some fruit. When we got into the light I discovered the pie was rhubarb. Well you couldn't carry that in a knapsack, so I ate it. By the time we had reached Vernal Falls the next morning about 4 A.M., I was sick. The pie was good, but no one should eat a whole pie. Especially rhubarb. I stayed with the crowd until they got to Little Yosemite and the branch-off trail and told them to go on, that I would wait for them at the top of Vernal Falls and go back to camp with them. They left me a small can, a handful of coffee, a few strips of bacon, and a few slices of bread, and then turned on up the trail. I told them it wasn't much further. It was all of eight miles or more and I didn't see them again until five o'clock, and plenty happened to me in the meantime.

I lay behind a rock and was awfully sick for most of the day. It was well afternoon before I felt well enough to get up and make my way back down the trail, to the locality of Vernal Falls.

The Emerald Pool and Silver Apron was such a pretty place. I decided to wait there, and by that time I realized that I would enjoy some coffee. So I looked around for somewhere to make

White and friends on a ledge, 1915. Courtesy of Yosemite National Park Archives.

a fire and boil the coffee and broil the bacon. I knew better but
I guess being so sick I wasn't thinking clearly. I saw a small hollow stump with a side limb just big enough to set the can on and
built the fire under it. Of course, that was no excuse. I was taken
sick again and when I came back from behind a bush, I saw what
I had done. The stump was blazing and the fire was spreading
among the pine needles. I dropped to the ground on my knees
and started to use my arm like a broom, sweeping the needles
to the front of me and to the side, and around that fire I went
until I had a space four feet wide scraped down to the dirt. Then
I went to the creek and filled my hat and made many trips until I
had that fire inside that circle really out. I even swabbed out the
inside of the stump. The scare stopped the sickness, and I felt
terribly guilty. I was sitting on a log wondering what to do next,
when a woman and a man and little boy came by. They neither
spoke to me nor offered any help. They could see I was alone
and I must have looked awful. She saw only the blackened area
where the fire had been. The woman looked back to her husband
and said, "When I get back to camp, I am going to report this."
Which no doubt she did.

I had had no food since the night before and was exhausted
and dirty. I went down to the stream and washed as best I could.
I had promised to wait near the trail till the others had returned.
I remembered what Bill had said about the speed and danger of
the Silver Apron. (Later a girl was washed off her feet at that very
place and carried over the falls.) So I went upstream a bit till I
saw a little islet covered with azaleas. I waded over to it, crawled
in under the bush, lay down, and went to sleep. I must have slept
about two hours when I was awakened by a horse's hoofs kick-
ing against rocks, and I scrambled to my feet and looked into the
barrel of a big pistol.

"You again. What are you doing now?" a ranger said crossly.
"Curled up in that khaki, you looked just like a mountain lion

and I was just about to take a shot at it. Being it was too close to where the tourists walk around."

He rode on after I had explained why I was there, I am sure that he saw the burned-over area but also must have seen that I had done a good job putting it out. I had saved one area of the park only to almost set another area on fire. That was guilt punishment enough for me.

I found a good rock projection where I could watch the falls as well as the trail and be seen by them, and sat down to wait the group's return.

"What in the world did you do all day by yourself?" they asked when they came back.

"Nothing much," I answered. How could I tell them that I had sat there filled with self-pity. That I had found you can be unhappy anywhere. I was lonesome for Camp Curry and the old gang. I missed hearing Mr. Curry, I wanted to comfort Mother Curry and didn't know how. I was tired of eating spoiled food, of sleeping in a barracks where you heard fifty girls all talking at once, and I was tired of quarreling among the help, and never having a cent of my own. I was tired of having the guests look at me as though I was something the cat had drug in. I was tired of working, I wanted to go back to school like other kids did. I was tired of being a dumbbell. I was seventeen and so very tired. I had lain down on that slab of granite about six miles from camp and cried a barrel of tears. What I had been through was as nothing to what was coming, and if I had known it, I might have cried another barrel or two of tears. Being young, of course I survived, but I am sure I must have learned something from that long, lonesome day.

The next day in the laundry Gene was almost killed. She was "saved by a hair," the boss told her. Someone on the feeder side of the mangle had let more than one sheet get away from her and the bunched-up wad of cloth got caught in the rollers and it dislodged the two-foot iron rod that was supposed to balance something and it flew backward, missing Gene's head by a fraction. She had jumped when she saw it coming. It grazed her shoulder enough to bruise it, but not to fracture it. We began to wonder if we had a jinx on us.

We heard that a large number of people from a newspaper convention in San Francisco were arriving Saturday evening, and that the camp would be crowded. Most of us went over to the Village in the evening to watch them come in. There was a recruiting bus standing by the post office, and a man sat by the table signing up the volunteers. To my surprise, Harry went over and signed up. He must have known what was going to happen later that night and wanted no part of it. He just signed up, boarded the bus, yelled he would write, waved, and was gone. A few days later I got a card saying he was on his way to France. I never heard from him again.

The buses came in loaded with tourists and to our surprise a big crowd was going back on the same buses. We didn't know then that every cook, busboy, and waitress from the camp were in that crowd.

The next morning the laundry was closed down, and we were all ordered over to the dining room to work until more help could be gotten from the cities.

I had never heard of a strike and it made little sense as to what was going on. I had carried little trays in the candy store but to be put in such a madhouse and given a huge tray to carry on my shoulder over the heads of hundreds of people scared me to pieces. I couldn't even find my station after I had gone to the kitchen. All those people looked alike to me. And everyone screaming at once and finally the girl in charge told me to get out and stay out until the laundry was opened again.

I was so glad, I would have run from the place if I could have. I went out and tramped the Valley just as I had done in 1915. I had only one bit of trouble and that was my own fault. I could not have blamed anyone but me.

I had never been up on El Capitan, and thought I would try it. I followed a trail, and when it seemed to disappear I decided to go back. I had no wish to get caught out on that mountain and be as cold as I had been before. I had used poor judgment, for I had brought neither food nor water nor matches. I started back but I could not find the trail. It was still light and I could see camp below, but I got terribly thirsty. I found a little pocket of water and although it didn't look good I let myself believe that if I didn't swallow it, it wouldn't hurt me. I'd just moisten my mouth. It tasted awful, and before I reached Yosemite Falls Trail I was feeling dizzy and was stumbling. I made it down to camp finally and near one of the faucets was a quart pitcher. I slumped down and drank that pitcher dry twice. I was awfully sick all night, but wouldn't tell Gene why, but I learned after that to drink either clean water or none.

The next evening while sitting in one of the guest chairs I looked up and there was Will, Bill's friend of 1915. We had a wonderful visit. He told me Bill had had to give up his hopes of college and was working and expected to go into service soon in the Communication Division. Pinkie was back in Kentucky. Camp Curry wasn't the same. There were no tricks this year. Everyone missed Mr. Curry too much. The camp was in mourning, and Mother Curry was doing her best to hold the camp. They had had over 11,000 guests in 1915 and more the next year and maybe still more this year. He was going on with his schooling and expected to teach someday. All in all, it was the nicest thing that had happened to me that season.

One of those free afternoons, I sauntered over to the platform where a piano was, and seeing the cover open I sat down to play a few little pieces. A man from the office came over, put the cover down, locked it, and said, "Naughty, naughty, mustn't touch." And went back to the office. I was aware that the camp was having troubles, maybe many that I had never heard of, but why should the help be so mean to each other? I had so much to learn, and I was to see much worse in the years to come. I got off the platform and took another walk.

A few days after the new set of helpers, waitresses, cooks, and others, arrived and the routine was reestablished. The laundry had to work harder to make up for the lost time and in a few days the equipment broke down completely. The only good thing about it was that most of the tourists had to get home to get children back to school, but even so there was some laundry to do.

Mrs. Curry was asked if she would take care of their laundry for the rest of the season and she agreed on one condition, that Gene and I would come up to help. We were happy.

Mother Curry put us in a guest tent and the few weeks that we spent there were joyous even though I met only a few that I had known in 1915. Everything was subdued. I never left camp once. I just was perfectly content to do my work, and eat good food, and sit by the fireplace and think and dream all I could. Somehow, I felt that I would not be back. I was right in that it was a long time, more than thirty years.

I took my boy back to work for a summer. I wanted him to learn to love my Valley. He had grown up on my stories and expected to find some fun up there, but two wars had sobered people. Workers worked. He found some old timers that had been at Curry's in 1915 and he said they had told him there had never been a year like it.

He went to Glacier Point and went out on the rock. The ranger said, "Can't you read the sign, boy? You're not to go beyond the railing."

"Mister, my grandmother stood on that rock, and so did my mother. Do you think I am not going to try?" The ranger took the camera and took a picture of him on the rock.

Later he had a Sunday off, and Saturday afternoon he went to the ranger station to get a permit to make a climb. "No, you can't go up Half Dome, the cables are broke down, and it's forbidden."

"Mister, my mother went up that Half Dome on a clothesline, the first woman to go up since 1875. I came up here to go up there." He got his permit, and slept up there that night.

I tried to find out if he had had any trouble going up or down, all he would say that it was awful cold. He was up 9,000 feet and nothing to break the wind. I'll bet he was cold even in a sleeping bag.

About the only thing he told me about was a trip he made to the Village on a bicycle at night when he realized a small bear was running along beside him as a dog might do. He said he wasn't too sure just how long that would keep up or what the bear had on his mind. Then a car came along and put on the high beam and gave him the horn and the bear ran off into the weeds.

I have a picture of my daughter leaning on the railing at Glacier Point, looking over, but she said she could take it or leave it.

If my story of a little girl who had so little gave you any laughs, and helped you see one beautiful drop of diamond glitter in the Valley falls, I will deem myself well paid.

It was close to thirty-five years before I went back again, as a tourist. I couldn't find Jungle Town. There was a larger auditorium. There were modern restrooms, there was a little round circle of rocks where the big, friendly fire had been. The guests of the land sat on stiff-backed benches, hundreds of them, just like in any movie house, with professionals to entertain them. The roof of the big cave had fallen in.

I walked into the office, and the clerks looked glassy-eyed from checking maybe a thousand persons in or out for the day. Cars whizzed by on the roads, hard surfaced like any highway. The meadow was no meadow any longer. It was a public campground, with campers crowded against each other. I was heartsick.

I went to sit on one of the log seats by the entrance facing the road. Even the top of North Dome looked like it was cracking up, large slabs of granite looked like they were ready to fall. Would they just slide off slowly or come crashing down with a roar and boom to scare the wits out of the guests in the million-dollar Awanhee, so snug, so fenced in under the Arches.

I turned to give my attention to the real challenger of the Valley, Half Dome. It seemed bigger than I had remembered. Had it grown or had I shriveled? I looked at the mountain of granite above me and said to myself, "You ol' fool, if you did write about it, nobody would believe it." And I thought of one of Mr. Curry's answers to the guests who would ask him if they should climb the mountain: "Madam, if you did, you'll wish you hadn't, if you don't, you'll wish you had."

If I wrote it, I may wish I hadn't, if I didn't, I may wish I had.

So I have written my story. I am sure the people of today are happy in their way, that they may not oh and ah and talk to strangers as we did, and they have to go faster to do everything, but maybe they can take in more in less time, so why should I judge them as I have been judged, even by little folks? Once I was sitting out of the wind behind a sand dune at a beach, a little three-year-old ran around it, took one look at me, and raced back. I heard her call out to her mother, "Oh, Mother, I just saw the Old Lady that lived in a shoe." I may have judged you wrongly. Please come and enjoy my Valley and bring your children and your grandchildren and all of you remember to thank John Muir, who gave you Yosemite, and remember Billie, who made it possible for you to get to the top of Half Dome.